IAN PORT

A Countryman's Tales of Yesteryear

'Appen Along. All in a Day's Work.

To My Darling Mary, The Golden Years

Life is like a mystery tour; it may not go the way you thought or may not be where you expected to go. The important thing is to enjoy the ride, the company and the beer.

ANON: BUT OFTEN REPEATED

Contents

Preface

Accompanied by the backdrop of the beautiful British landscape, A Countryman's Tales of Yesteryear takes you on a gentle amble through memories of the Golden Years from 1947 to 1967. Recounting tales and anecdotes, you are invited to join lively and colourful communities moving on from post-war Britain, through to the 'slightly swishing sixties' of rural Hampshire. You meander through villages with the quaint stone cottage, historic pubs, and communities where the river provides a focal point. Acres of fields bring rural scenery to life, surrounded by rolling green hills, with little streams flowing through as they pass by railway stations, churches, and schools.

You will cross paths with joiners, builders, farmers, publicans, shopkeepers, gamekeepers, blacksmiths and rectors, and tumble upon many other strong characters at the heart of the community. With a passion for nature, and embracing the outdoor life, the author's fascination for the stillness and wonder of the countryside will entertain and enthral.

Imagine the author as he rapidly approaches his Eightieth birthday. He sits by the fireside with a pipe and glass of malt whisky and recalls some antics of his youth. Some will not be politically correct - that concept is yet to come into existence. A few will be morally dubious, if not positively illegal. Money was in pounds, shillings and pence, and Europe was a mysterious place where wars had only just ended, and men recently returned. As the evening draws on, with more whisky consumed, the tone of the anecdotes may deteriorate. The odd swear word may creep in, as the author's companions and workmates may become a little more disreputable. However, the whisky is smooth and mellow, so the tales will not seem too outrageous.

A few names have been changed to save embarrassment, although most of the people are sadly no longer with us. The author wishes to jog memories, reminisce and to share the nostalgia, atmosphere and the charisma of the time. He hopes his tales will amuse, entertain and offer you cheer and delight. Most are stand-alone chapters, and a 'Countryman's Tales of Yesteryear' is a book to dip into, to sip like a mellow malt, and smile tolerantly over.

Ian raises a glass to the memories of those, the likes of whom we will never see again.

Acknowledgement

Mary, my wife for appearing in the tales and supporting me since.

Jeanette, my daughter, without whom this book would never have been produced and who added polish where needed.

The vast cast of characters, reprobates and good friends who unwittingly provided the raw material.

Thank you, one and all.

1

Conkers and Kings

It was less than a mile up the hill, past the church and across the village
green. It was a short walk in the tender, summerlike months, but a drag
in the more frequent dismal murk. Today, I walked along hand-in-hand
with Rita, a grown-up girl of ten who lived next door. 'Course you'll like it,
Ian' she assured me, yet I remained unconvinced. But as I admired Rita from
afar, I would give it a go! Not that I had a choice - what sort of place would
not let my dog accompany me?

'Right, 'ere ya goes'. I looked up at Ria, my mentor and the custodian of
my sandwiches. The school was a small, brick-built, Victorian building with
two classrooms. It seemed massive and daunting to me, though. Rita led
me, as I weakly protested, through the noisy playground. The sound struck
me like a solid wall after the quiet of the farm where I lived. The smell of
the school with wet coats, floor polish and generations of small children
in various degrees of cleanliness added to my fears. We entered the school
through a cloakroom with huge iron coat-pegs festooned with coats and
satchels; I had neither of these, and I now felt more out of place than ever.
My lunch was a cheese sandwich, no crisps, sweets were on ration and kept
for special occasions. Rita had my sandwich, with strict instructions not to
let me have it until mid-day - very wise, as I would have eaten it on the way
to school.

Once I reached the classroom, I found myself levered from Rita's hand,

and I stood enthralled by a calendar hanging on an otherwise bleak wall. The calendar had a beautifully drawn hedgerow scene showing the birds, animals and wild plants appropriate to the season. Lost and caught-up in the scenery, an older boy, pulled me to a desk and back to reality with a thud—time to begin my formal education. In came Miss Vine, an ancient person, much older than my Mum and Dad, she must have been at least forty-five. The entire class shot to their feet and chorused, 'G' morninmiss'. No answer. I never recall her answering. She would glower at us over a pair of glasses, slam open a register and fill it with a neat series of diagonal strokes that reminded me of the pattern on a pheasant's feather. Woe betides any poor child who spoilt the pattern with an 'O' for absent.

I don't recall any lessons either. I remember the milk break, though. We'd collected our milk from the dairy on the farm in quart enamelled jugs, and now each small bottle had round cardboard tops with a pop-out section to push a straw through. We kept the tops, making sure we put aside this treasure for washing and to save for some ritual the older children performed in handicraft. It intrigued me. That first morning droned on, as did many more to follow.

I learned what was happening outside of the classroom was far more interesting than what took place within the walls. I gazed out of the classroom window, feeling true envy for the milkman. He ambled through the village on a milk cart pulled by a grey pony as old as himself. He seemed to not have a care as his cigarette dangled from his lip, and a wave for everyone. Dressed in his white coat, peaked cap and with his battered leather money-bag strapped at a diagonal across his body, he trundled his round. To me, it looked the best job in the world. When it rained the small wooden cab kept the worst of the drizzle off, but he was free, unlike the little unhappy prisoners. The latter were sitting chanting, "Twotwosurfur", "Twothreesarsix", or a similar foreign language.

That first day, it seemed hours had passed before Rita came to rescue me with my curled cheese sandwich and a peck on my cheek. The day seemed so long. Surely, they didn't expect me to come here every weekday? Slowly, I learned to conform to the strange rituals of school in a time when designer labels or play stations did not measure status. For a while, marbles would be king of the currency. We traded small dull clay marbles, won, fought over, and even stolen from classmates until we gained enough to trade-up for coloured glass beauties. These, we would hold up to the light and marvel at the jewel-like colours and admire the swirl,like cigarette smoke in a small sapphire globe with twisting planes of abstract emerald. We would hurl these with no regard for their beauty, down the dusty asphalt until we won enough to swap them for 'Joeys.' The ultimate in prize marbles - twice the size, twice the brilliance, twice the danger. Inevitably, a larger boy would punch us hard enough to persuade us to hand them over. Never cry! This would be the ultimate disgrace. Allowing yourself to be robbed was bad. To be robbed and labelled a cry baby was a social disaster.

As the autumn term laboured on, Marbles gave way to Conkers! On the way home from school, we would scrabble through the fallen green, spiky pods and break them open with the occasional yelp of pain as a spike cautioned us. The pristine shining splendour of a newly opened chestnut, glistening like newly varnished mahogany, never ceased to impress me. They soon went dull, and we threaded them onto a string. Or for the really affluent, leather bootlaces gained from older brothers or fathers. As the days drew in, we covered the playground with shattered brown husks as we battled. Boy against boy, conker against conker, until slowly the days would shorten, and the mists would thicken.

Then the first frosts came and hardened until the inside of window panes were white with frozen patterns of ferns and exotic white plumes. I shivered in my unheated bedroom, teeth chattering as I pulled on my short grey flannel trousers; we all wore short trousers until we went to the 'big school' at eleven, a distant and daunting prospect. Very few of us had indoor sanitation, and a wash meant the kitchen sink or an enamel bowl on a stand. We never had running cold water. Ours came from a well by the back door. Lovely to drink in the summer, not that bad in the winter. We had the luxury of an enormous kitchen range. Two massive kettles of water would hiss steam and bubble away. One of them was too big for me to lift, so I used the smaller one, filling it from the galvanised bucket in the outhouse. It was a proud day for me when I was big enough to make the trip to the well myself — but shortly afterwards we were 'modernised'. Delighted, my mother had a pump in the kitchen! Indoor water! It came from the same well, of course, through a cast iron pump with a huge bent handle. It was a sullen, reluctant brute that needed priming with a cup full of water. Frantic clanging effort would produce a reluctant belch of rust, followed by sporadic gushes. My father swore that tea never tasted the same and furtively filled the kettle with water from the well.

Winter brought some compensation. We would run to school swinging a cocoa tin on a piece of string around our necks. With several holes punched in the container and smouldering rags inside glowing red, it saved our hands from the nippiness. We gratefully grasped the tin between mitten'd fingers until the wool scorched and the feeling returned to fingers, blue with cold. When the frost was heavy, we made a slide in the playground—a shining ribbon of glass with whooping children hurtling down. A few would fall over, and they were hauled into the classroom to have iodine dabbed upon bloodied limbs. The cure was usually worse than the injury and ensured that only the badly hurt would be foolish enough to catch the eagle eye of the Head Mistress.

Inside the building, the school was warm. Smelly perhaps, but warm. An enormous pot-bellied, coke-fuelled stove stood by the side of the teacher's raised oak desk. A wire surround protected it from us, or perhaps us from it, and we would hang our dripping coats from this to dry during lessons. The stove was nearly as tall as me, but I could see the legend 'slow but sure' cast into the top with a tortoise symbol underneath. The brave or reckless would spit onto the nearly red-hot top to watch the small globule leap across until it vanished with the last pop. This was courage. Or perhaps, foolhardiness. Miss Vine would catch any offender by the ear and drag them in front of the class to administer summary justice with a cane. Pupils reluctant to hold out their hand had any available part of the body lashed upon. This taught us only to spit surreptitiously.

Often the strain of attempting to teach her reluctant charges would prove too much for Miss Vine, and she would scream, 'I am reaching the end of my

4

tether.' This always made me think of the mangy old nanny goat tethered at the end of our lane. She would then fling herself into her chair and cross her legs, allowing us an alarming glimpse of long Eau- de- Nil bloomers and thick lisle stockings.

Just as winter seemed without end, snowdrops suddenly caught us by surprise, and the mood would change. Small bunches of violets would appear on the teacher's desk, followed by primroses and daffodils. The boys fished tadpoles out of the small muddy pond that lay almost opposite the school and filled jam jars with a mixture of pond water, debris and little confused, black, wiggling 'taddies.' The taddies sat in a pot on the windowsill until they grew legs. We then dumped them back into the pond to become frogs. The fully grown frogs would send their sons and daughters to the village school the following spring!

Then came the magic sound of spring, 'Cuckoo, Cuckoo.' It appeared everyone waited for spring to foretell and predict our upcoming year's fortune. And we would gaze wistfully out of the small-paned window at the sun-dappled pond. Agitated moorhens scuttled across, and dragonflies darted, their iridescent bodies like slivers of coloured glass as they shimmered in an aerial dance. Swallows swooped for a beak-full of mud for their urgent housing projects. Eventually, even the hardened teacher would succumb and suggest a nature ramble. A minor victory at last, and a brief glimpse of freedom before incarceration in the gloomy school again. We took advantage of our temporary freedom by flicking dried cowpats at each other and similar experiments, hoping horse flies would select a victim other than ourselves to torture. What fun! And this is how our year progressed. Some variances with the weather, but time rolled on.

I must have learnt something. The chanting of times tables perhaps, although I totally could not connect this to maths and I remained almost innumerate at school. I could read, as my father had taught me before I started school. There was nothing in infants for me. I had read the offerings, so I borrowed books where I could. I read anything, Enid Blyton, of course, textbooks, sauce-bottle labels, anything. Geography was an excuse to read, and I roamed the veldt, explored tundra and galloped over dusty deserts on flea-bitten camels. In history, I marched with the legions and pulled the arrow from Harold's eye. I might have been at Runnymede too, but I was never required! This didn't matter, as examinations were 'not for the likes of us'. This was the mantra.

* * *

I knew one girl who passed her eleven plus, Mary, the sister of Rita, my guardian angel. Mary was sixteen, a total adult to me, and she had beauty and brains. They lived in a cottage close to us on the farm. I called her father, Uncle Geoff, and this was a courtesy title, as was normal with family friends. He was a tall, placid, kindly man, and a gardener at the 'big house' as we called the manor.

His wife was 'Aunt' Betty, who worked as a housemaid with my mother at the 'big house'. They treated me as one of the family, and the girls treated me like a puppy. They shared homemade toffee, wiped the sticky remains off my face and sat me between them to snuggle up and go to sleep on their ancient sofa. Meanwhile, things carried on as normal at school - they explained nothing. I'd heard of televisions, but nobody that I knew had seen one. I put them in the same category as unicorns and other mythological creatures. We had the 'wireless set' as we then called the radio, and I remember the excitement when we bought our first 'mains set'. Before this we had an accumulator - this looked like an oblong glass fish tank. We charged this at regular intervals and leads wound their way to our wireless, and we festooned another length of wire off the picture rail to act as an aerial. The term 'wireless' totally confused me - we had wires going in all directions!

We would listen to the carefully enunciated, clipped tones of the news-reader as he announced that the Glorious Gloucesters had crossed the thirty-eighth parallel in Korea. Nobody told me what this meant, and I thought that a parallel could be a river or perhaps a vast bank. Convinced that this was a prominent feature of the landscape, I visualised our troops 'going over the top' just as the soldiers had in the first World War. Adult programmes were not for us. We had 'Childrens' Hour' or as a special treat, 'Dick Barton,

Special Agent'. One evening, I sneaked downstairs to listen at the sitting-room door to a new programme called 'The Archers.' All the adults were talking about the new show, so in my reckoning, I'd risk the castigation, but I rapidly became bored. With no mention of Robin Hood or Sherwood Forest, I quickly lost interest and went back to bed shivering and disillusioned.

Although I had no pocket money, it was no great hardship as I could not buy sweets because of rationing. But every larder contained home-made cake. The orchards were full of apples. Laden with berries, we foraged hedgerows, making the most of all nature's offerings. I was lucky. My parents bought me a comic every week. I soon realised that I could swap after reading and started taking two old comics and a penny in exchange. This meant I could read the Beano, Dandy, and to top it off, The Eagle. Dan Dare decimated the evil Mekon, his jutting jaw looking more formidable than his radical ray gun, and he earned me a few pence into the bargain.

'The grey post-war years' did not exist for me - I remember buoyant celebrations. The Festival of Britain, pretty princesses marrying dashing naval officers, and we commemorated with a real firework display when their son and heir was born. The last was truly memorable for me. The soldier son of a neighbour 'borrowed' some signal flares and rockets from his unit, together with some thunderflashes, a giant 'banger' used for grenade practice. This enlivened an already impressive local display and dropped the milk yield on our farm by several gallons.

My strongest memory is the sad one. Confined to bed with some childish ailment and the radio for comfort, half-listening, I heard the announcement. "The king is dead, long live the king." Confused, I staggered downstairs yelling the news. 'The king is dead'. No one believed me. They thought I was delirious, or maybe I had been listening to a radio play. When at last they tried playing with the tuning knobs, tapping the silent brown bakelite wireless, nothing. Silence. Transmission was suspended.

The end of an era.

2

End of an Era

F ollowing the loss of our King, adults were subdued, but as children, we never realised that things were changing, and life carried on much as before. That was the thing back then. As children, we held a privileged position where our younger years developed independence, resilience, and tenacity, and we did this through policing ourselves. We learnt mostly through our mistakes but living in the village gave us plenty of opportunities to explore and discover. Mostly we made our own amusement. In the pleasant weather, we had immense amounts of freedom, and we had the run of the village and the surrounding fields. During the long light summer holidays, we took our jam sandwich and a bottle of homemade lemonade and disappeared all day. Our parents did not expect us home, quite the opposite.

Sometimes we would follow the stream as it meandered through meadows, yellow with buttercups. Then we kicked off our sandals and waded through the gravelly shallows or felt the mud ooze between our toes as the smell of wild mint filled the air. When we sat quietly, glimpses of a flashing electric blue kingfisher rewarded us. The bird gave us a brief display of its flying skills before folding its wings and plunging into the water to emerge with a glistening silver fish in its dripping bill. The stream was central to many of our adventures as we built barges, bridges and dams.

One of our gang's mother tried to put us off the attractions of the stream by telling us vaguely that it was 'full of germs.' This had the effect of increasing the rivers mesmerising draw and appeal. For many weeks we patrolled the banks with homemade spears and sharpened sticks on a germ hunt and quest. We didn't know exactly what we were looking for. But our imagination turned any weed-covered stone or piece of branch, twig or stick into a deadly germ and we would massacre it. We whooped and hollered like Red Indians as we skewered our foe. Don, my dog, was the quietest and most gentle of animals, but he loved a good germ hunt. He would leap into the water, growling and snarling before bounding back out onto the bank and administering the Coupe de Grace to his quarry. He would shake himself vigorously and shower us with silver droplets before we sat down and shared our sandwiches with him, congratulating ourselves on another victory.

From time to time, we walked down to the next village. The road was near-silent, and we rarely saw a car. Our road wound through a wooded area for about a mile with grassy banks rising steeply each side. In early spring, violets thrived, and later primroses and celandines were so thickly spaced that the banks really looked as though some eccentric had carpeted them. After about another half a mile, the banks broadened into a grassy plain and our excitement would mount as we reached our goal. This was an airfield separated from the road by barbed wire which gave an unrestricted view of the runway. The RAF used it for training on twin-engine aircraft. On most days, the Anson and Oxford aircraft would take off and fly a few circuits before practising its approach, wobbling toward the runway like fledgeling rooks. Their engine note rising and falling and tails yawing or sailing gracefully in like mature swans before touching down and rolling a few yards along the tarmac, before opening their throttle and taking off again. They called this 'circuits and bumps.

Although this was about six years following the war, those who'd lived through-it kept the memory afresh. Stories in comics and the tales of our elders fed our imaginations. Because of this, all of us boys longed to see a Spitfire. We credited any single-engine aircraft with this accolade. Until the day came when two sleek, elliptically winged planes swept down the runway with a snarling, throbbing roar from their Merlin engines. The craft left us in no doubt that our dream had come true. The two magnificent planes swept low over our heads as we leapt up and down, waving frantically. Then to our delight, the aircraft turned and swept low over the airfield and waggled their wings before streaking into the clouds and vanishing. We remained looking up at the skies, but they did not return, although we could hear the distinctive note of the engine for some time. And convinced that the 'salute' was for our benefit, we knew we would never forget. By the time we went back to school, we had exaggerated this and described a squadron of Spitfires performing a full display for our benefit. But I now know it is more likely that they were saluting some of their comrades on the airfield.

* * *

Throughout the country, there was an acute housing shortage. The enemy bombing destroyed many houses, and despite council house building, there were nowhere near enough homes to go round. Many families shared or took in lodgers, but some families had no option but to occupy old wartime huts that were no longer needed by the services. We knew these families as squatters, and there were many of them. Although some stigma to being a squatter and living in a hut, may have existed, I did not see any. In fact, as a child, I envied many of them who lived very close to the airfield. One family lived in the body of a giant troop-carrying glider, which they had converted into a very comfortable home. This was larger than any caravan I had ever seen. And I was green with envy when I saw that one bedroom was in the old cockpit, reached via a short ladder. No doubt it had its drawbacks and was difficult to heat in the winter. But it looked very cosy with a coal-burning stove and a flue poking up through the fuselage.

The older men would wear suits to visit the seaside, or perhaps sports coats and grey flannel trousers. Most of the younger men would have open-necked shirts but still wore highly polished shoes. The women were in flowery summer dresses, and we boys wore khaki shorts and either an Aertex shirt or a 'sloppy joe', a sort of tee-shirt. There was no branding or display of labels, and subsequently, no peer pressure to conform to the latest fashion. But there was one exception - the 'must-have' item. This was an elasticised belt with the clasp in the form of a snake that passed through a loop. It didn't matter what colour the belt was, as long as you flaunted the S-shaped chrome snake.

The other item of clothing that united us was the swimsuit, no matter what colour it was, it shared one characteristic; it was knitted. This still baffles the generation that invented the jet engine, radar and penicillin. We persisted in wearing knitted swimsuits and accepted the tradition in the same way as the Emperor's New Coat. The knitted material was not some exotic material designed to repel water. No, they purled the knitted swimsuit out of last year's pullover. And this was the same sweater that became twice as heavy, twice as baggy, and very uncomfortable when washed. So, who on earth conceived wearing a garment like this to swim in? As soon as the swimmer left the safety of the water, the soggy, misshapen garment would attempt to head back to the water without its owner. Teeth chattering, the hapless victim would stagger up the beach frantically clutching the sagging waistband.

Meanwhile, the heavy, saturated gusset was determinedly heading for the kneecaps, leading to a feeling of intense insecurity. With dry land finally reached, the victim could sink gratefully down onto the beach. Although sand and wet wool made an uncomfortable bedfellow, we'd enthusiastically pack our bathers for the following year, benefitting from the fact that they had grown.

As the sun went down, the coach arrived. A group of sunburned or windburned, tired and happy people would climb onto the coach which chugged off home to the accompaniment of the same old songs each time. 'Ten Green Bottles', 'She'll Be Coming 'Round the Mountains' and 'Molly Malone'. With faces burning from sun, wind or memories of woollen swimsuits, the youngsters sleepily leant against parents, or each other, in contented litters. Halfway home, the coach would draw into a pub car park. As a last treat, our parents would buy a packet of Smiths crisps with salt in a blue twist of paper and a bottle of Vimto. The men would have their beer or cider, and the more daring among the women ordered up a port and lemon. Soon the red faces of the adults became even more flushed. Elbows nudged ribs. Women giggled, and many jokes made that went right over our heads as our parents let their hair down. Finally, the coach would grind out of the car park on the last leg home. Most of us slept despite the increasing volume of the song until someone would come round with the hat holding a collection for the driver. The song would turn to 'For he's a Jolly Good Fellow', but few of us sleepy youngsters remember being carried happily home.

Ian and Don

3

Dreaming of a White Christmas

'**D**o you believe in Father Christmas?' Johnny inquired anxiously, wiping his nose on the back of his fingerless mittens. His gloves, knitted from reclaimed khaki wool, now faded to a suitably organic shade that would warrant a romantic description in a modern colour chart, camouflaged his snot perfectly.

'Nah' I replied, a little cautiously, with fingers crossed like a modern agnostic on a plane with failing engines.

'If there is a Father Christmas, he is a miserable old sod. Think about it. All the toff kids get superb presents; all the poor ones get nutthin'. The rest of us get threatened with getting sod all if we're not good for the entire year... or probably the rest of our lives... maybe longer, I dunno!'

Johnny looked crestfallen. Not that I could see his crest. Hidden as it was under a balaclava, itself a strange-looking garment knitted from what was originally a red sweater and fading from a rusty pink on top to a mouldy beetroot under the chin. Strangely it matched his complexion as the cold blotched his mottled skin. Not convinced that I was right, I remained open-minded on this one. I tried being good for several days in a row once, and it made no difference to my presents that I could see.

The son of a wealthy farmer in the village made no effort and treated us with the same contempt that he showed his dog and sister. And, it was an amiable dog. He got a horse for Christmas, a real live horse. I almost believed in Santa Claus though, when the horse swayed too close to a gatepost and broke the lad's leg while they were out with the local hunt.

Johnny lived with his mother in an isolated cottage just beyond the village limits. His father had 'not come back from the war'. A phrase used to describe anything from 'killed in action' to disappearing with 'another woman'. No doubt the gossiping tongues in the village knew or at least invented a colourful story. However, it was 'not for children to know'. Their rented cottage had weather-beaten thatch with green moss-draped heavily in places like a rotting shroud. Heavy rain would mean dashing about placing buckets and bowls under the persistent drips. These would turn into constant streams, if not torrents, under stormy conditions. Johnny and his mother made light of this, 'See, we've got running water in our cottage, even if we have to go the well to fetch drinking water like you.'

Under hard frost conditions or periods of heavy snow, the roof would become weatherproof. Under a layer of ice the meagre heat given off by the smoky log fire was not enough to melt the crust of icing. However, this hardly ever happened at Christmas, as hard frosts and snows are a regular feature of January weather. Cold, dank, grey days are the hallmark of December, despite the pictures on Christmas cards. These descriptions in carols and warblers are more exports from America dreaming of a White Christmas. Johnny and his mother lived in their damp, cold and cramped cottage and struggled to pay the rent through the money that his mother earned by cleaning, washing and the odd job such as potato picking, so spare money was non-existent for luxuries such as Christmas presents. It was hard enough to find money for food. In years to come, the cottage was condemned, as were quite a few in the village - some of these still had earth floors, so they were more than due for an upgrade! Johnny and his mother eventually moved into one of the new council houses with inside sanitation and hot and cold running water.

I was one of the fortunate middle grounds of present receivers. I knew that there would be a Christmas stocking, in later years a Christmas pillowcase, containing an orange, sweets and a rare treat of chocolate money, each coin wrapped in glistening gold paper for all the world like the doubloons or pieces of eight in a pirate story. I would usually get a diary or drawing book with coloured pencils. Individually wrapped would be an annual or perhaps a Thomas the Tank Engine book and in later years an addition to my growing Meccano set. We could not afford a whole boxed set, so I built mine up. The Meccano magazine showed huge cranes and mighty bridges. Although I never gained enough to create the impressive crane or bridge that the makers illustrated, I still had enough to build my ideas of cars and trains and even a smaller crane that really worked. I showed this by lowering the budgie in its cage over the stairwell. Unsurprisingly, the budgie and my mother had a fit of the vapours. My mother confiscated the set for a week as they both recovered.

There would also be a 'big present.' This could be a new pullover knitted by my mother when she thought I was not looking, or a new pair of school shoes. It helped to confirm my suspicions about Santa Claus unless he frequented the same wool shop as my mother his tastes were remarkably similar. I had a bicycle. It was a sturdy, if somewhat elderly bike, in the old-fashioned 'sit up and beg style with rod operated brakes. I kept the rust off the chrome with generous amounts of elbow grease, and a damp rag dipped in sand. Any chrome left after my attempts at polishing I protected with three-in-one oil. It was not a pretty bike. It had dull black paintwork adorned with gold lines back in the nineteen-thirties and was now fading and non-existent in places. It had a saddle, lined and creased like a witch's face with a mouldering saddlebag attached. The saddle that is, not the witch's face. However, it had three-speed gears, a faithful Sturmey Archer arrangement built into the hub, with the short gear change lever mounted on the crossbar. This was no doubt designed by a sadist with a warped sense of humour.

The bike was a little too large for me, so coming to a halt meant straddling the crossbar before my feet would touch the floor. But because the speed was so slow, I wobbled and fell off. I would hit the crossbar and slide the length. Straddling the bar, until my slide stopped as a very delicate part of my anatomy snagged the gear lever that projected from the crossbar. Spectacular results occurred when standing up on the pedals to attempt a steep hill. Either the chain slipped, or a foot slipped off the pedals leading to high speed and noisy re-enactment of the not uncommon, painful means of dismounting previously described. I always thought an ex cyclist had coined the cliché, 'screaming to a halt,' with painful memories of the Sturmey Archer.

Johnny also had a bike. He had found a frame on a rubbish tip and helped by some older boys, he slowly built a bike out of assorted bits that other owners had abandoned. If a camel is a horse designed by a committee, then the same committee must have had a terrible day and designed Johnny's bike. Nothing quite matched, and the bike had several bits held on by fencing wire. It lacked a three-speed, which was probably a blessing in disguise. However, it had a fixed wheel - this meant that it was not possible to stop pedalling, as long as the wheels went round the pedals also continued to turn. This meant that the lack of brakes didn't matter, as Johnny could stand on the pedals and stop.

This sounds simple, but when I tried it, I launched myself, and propelled over the handlebars and landed in the road shortly before the bike ran me over. Johnny rushed towards me, his face contorted with concern, stroking his bike he then turned to me, 'can't see a mark on it.' He then curled up with laughter. 'You're in for it though, look at your torn trousers.'

One day just before Christmas we were walking because Johnny had a flat tyre, he tried borrowing my pump but no amount of vigorous pumping, puffing and panting would inflate his tyre. We'd combed all the well-known rubbish tips and could not find another wheel. He would have settled for a different sized wheel. Anything to get him mobile again, but our lengthy search was in vain that day and Johnny resigned himself to having to walk everywhere over the holiday. This meant missing a lot of fun because the rest of the boys were too heartless to restrict their own activities by walking. We plodded on, his mottled face a study in misery until we reached my gate and left Johnny to push his bike the extra mile home. I watched his muffled figure huddled over his bike with a flat tyre as he wheeled it slowly home, steam percolating through his disreputable balaclava and forming beads on the sodden wool.

The next day was Christmas Eve, and I didn't see Johnny until Boxing

Day. First thing Boxing day, actually before breakfast Boxing day, I heard a tinkling from a bicycle bell and looked out to see Johnny, mounted on his bike and frantically waving at me. I blinked, there was even a sprinkling of snow and a Robin sitting on the log where we put out crumbs for the birds. If the voice of Bing Crosby had appeared on our old brown bakelite radio, the picture would be complete. I rubbed some frost off the inside of the window and beckoned him in. He rushed through the door brandishing a small oval yellow tin. 'I've got one. See, I've got a present, told you there was a Father Christmas'. Johnny had the best present that he could imagine. A Dunlop puncture repair outfit.

Johnny became a mechanic and then opened a small garage from which he sold cars. He then moved into town. I am told that if you now go into the largest dealership in top of the market cars, and are fortunate enough to get an invitation into the managing director's office, you will find a dapper, smartly suited man sitting behind an expensive desk. Between a gold fountain pen and gold cigarette case, there is a slightly less golden but equally loved yellow tin. All the puncture repair patches are used, and all it contains is a very brown withered holly leaf.

4

Whale of a Time

I realise that I was very fortunate to have been born in the middle of a war. I was too young for the horrific events and trauma to affect me directly in my situation. And peace resumed when I had just reached an age when it may have impacted on me more.

For a child born in the 1940s, life after the war seemed ideal. It was very different for parents and anyone old enough to remember the pre-war days, though; many people expected life to resume as it was before. Some never got that this was not to be for many years into peacetime. I remember complaints about the lack of 'luxury items' such as bananas and chocolate and the shortage of 'real' meat. The children of my generation were blissfully unaware of what we were missing. We had been born into a world where these things did not exist. We were lucky.

I, for one, was ecstatic with faggots, meatloaf and spam fritters. On the rare occasions when sweets were available, I really enjoyed them without realising, or understanding, that before the war they were freely available. Unlike the days of ration coupons and cash, so we were grateful and endured none of the sense of frustration that our elders suffered from. We knew nothing else, and every small luxury re-gained a novelty, not one more step back to an age before and life as it used to be.

We had Easter eggs, and my oval, egg-shaped treat was a made of hard compressed cardboard nearly the size of a rugger ball. Covered with foil and silver paper saved from pre-war chocolates, I could separate the two halves of the egg to reveal a variety of home-made sweets, fudge, toffee and white mice moulded from icing sugar. If I was lucky and we had enough ration points left, there might be a few bought sweets too, maybe even some chocolate. My mother would store the cardboard egg carefully until the following year, ready to fill with more delights. The first time I saw a chocolate egg, I could not believe it.

Living in the country, we had no problem getting fresh eggs and took great pleasure in painting the shells in garish colours for our Easter breakfast. At parties and celebrations, the adults would sacrifice some of their 'points,' as they called the ration coupons, to make sure that we at least had jelly and cake in some form. A real treat was a soft bread roll with pink or white icing on top. I remember that there was a fashion for green jelly poured into a mould in the shape of a crouching rabbit. When set and turned out on a plate, it sat green and quivering, like an experiment in an animal laboratory that had gone badly wrong.

I can only speak from personal experience. It was probably very different in a city, but I noticed no real shortages or deprivation. Most people grew vegetables, potatoes were not on ration and were freely available in our village. We had the luxury of real eggs, although I also liked powdered egg. And eggs meant chickens, once the chicken passed its laying days. Perhaps our parents had been used to a different diet in the pre-war days, but the children of my generation were content. There was also a very relaxed attitude toward rules and regulations, and creative interpretation of laws helped supply most pantries. Many cottages had a shotgun hanging on the wall or propped behind the door. The general attitude was that the farmers would be grateful if a few rabbits finished up under pie crusts instead of eating valuable crops. No one asked the farmers, but as long as the rabbits were for eating, not selling a blind eye was turned. Old Jake summed this up, 'Ow can any bugger own a rabbit? It 'ops frum one field to another. One minute it's in my field. Next, it's in his when it's going under the wire does its tail belong to me and its ears belong to him?"

There was a mystical source of exotic delights that the adults would describe in hushed tones as the black market. I visualised an Arabian souk, a street full of stalls groaning under the weight of delicacies and luxuries, the canvas covers over the stalls pitch black and flapping gently in the breeze. Look as I might, I never found this market, but every so often something would arrive from this mystical place. Adults would hold a finger to lips as they exchanged looks with eyes sparkling with delight. It was highly illegal and could lead to heavy fines or even imprisonment. But Uncle Stan summed up the feeling of the times when he said 'I didn't sit freezing my arse off in a gun turret, ten thousand feet over Germany with Jerry bullets whistling 'round me, to be told that my Missus can't have a new pair of knickers'

I wasn't overkeen on some attempts to give us protein. For example, there was a large quantity of whale meat around. Now the Japanese might regard this as a delicacy. I can only imagine that they use a different cookbook to my mother. The taste still lingers; it can truly be said that it is neither fish, flesh, nor fowl. My poor mother tried to make it palatable but to no avail. According to the Government hand out it was suitable for all forms of cooking apart from roasting. I have got no doubt that the person who wrote that sat slapping his thighs with laughter as he ate his roast pheasant and regaled his dinner companions with the story. I may be wrong. Perhaps a Japanese prisoner of war wrote it, extracting revenge for Nagasaki.

Marinating it overnight in vinegar, we smothered it with onions. We minced it and incorporated it into a meatloaf, which was always the last desperate resort for unidentifiable meat. The result was the same—stewed wellington boot in a sauce of seawater, with a faint taste of diesel oil. Perhaps the whale meat we received resulted from a massive collision between mammal and ship, and some enterprising sailor had rescued the dead whale from the wreckage.

Many wartime recipes were still being used, and some of them were very good, at least we thought so. But then we were not used to the real thing so items such as carrot marmalade might have made the adults shudder, but it made a welcome addition to our diet.

I believe that they lifted the rationing on chocolate in 1949. I had had a Mars bar before, but I had never seen an entire bar eaten in one session. We grew up with the belief, 'you'll be sick if you eat it all', and never once did we question. However, we watched in amazement as one boy ate his way from one end to another and held our breaths, waiting for him to be violently ill, as predicted by our elders. Much to my disappointment, he survived. Rita carefully cut hers into seven portions so she could have one every day but was so soft-hearted that she shared hers with us. So, the bar only lasted minutes, not days. But it was all too good to be true. There had been a miscalculation, and they re-imposed rationing, and this survived for a few more years. We accepted this. Life was easier, and there was no point in complaining. We got a clip on the ear and were told to stop whinging.

* * *

Clothing was simple. We wore grey flannel shorts. If you were fortunate enough to have new ones, they would be a couple of sizes too large and flapped below your knees, and the waistband would be gathered in a series of pleats. After a year or two they would fit perfectly, then finally they would come halfway up your chapped, and reddened legs and the waistband would strain to go around your middle. By now they would have also collected a series of darns and patches. Everyone else looked like this too, and no one commented. In fact, the only time that any teasing took place was when a boy arrived wearing a brand-new pair of shorts which fitted! We also wore a grey flannel shirt. We have lost the art of making shirts like this. There was some strange ingredient that lingered from the days of hair shirts. They itched anywhere it contacted the skin. Most of these were also grey, but I don't believe that they started that way.

So, there was a little grey army going reluctantly to school? Not quite, there was a mania for knitting. So-called 'fair isle' pullovers were all the rage and mothers knitted these from many colours of wool in a bright and varied pattern. They all had one thing in common; they were 'original'. They were original, alright. In fact, they had originally been another garment. Mothers used to sit and unravel woollen garments that were no longer serviceable and use the odd wool to knit these pullovers. It had the advantage of using up every old scrap of yarn and lending a bit of colour to life at the same time. There must have been a pattern available, but there was no evidence of this in the bands of colours, zig-zags diamonds and other geometric marvels that graced the playground. They would use any scrap of wool that did not find its way into the pullover for balaclava helmets and strange fingerless gloves. I swear that some boys who resembled multi-coloured caterpillars until the summer holidays would emerge from their cocoon, blink in the sunshine, and take cover again in September.

There were no trainers back then, of course. Schoolwear comprised a stout pair of leather shoes or boots sometimes. These would inevitably have leather soles which fathers tipped with small crescents of steel like miniature horseshoes at toe and heel. Every family that I knew had a shoe last at home, a sort of cast-iron spider with spindly legs and different sized feet which could be turned over to give a range of shoe sizes. The idea was to repair shoes that had a hole worn in the sole by placing them upside down on one of the metal feet of the shoe last and applying a new sole. Often with a 'Philips stick-a-sole' - a rubber sole trimmed to size and stuck onto the roughened leather with a strong-smelling adhesive. Bought is various sizes and nailed in place, new heels replaced the levered off worn heels, bringing boots back to life. One lesson quickly learned was never to laugh at a girl wearing old, patched boots. She either had a large brother who was the original owner, or a sensitive father; both options were equally painful to the mickey taker.

The other universal item of footwear was the gym shoe. Physical education was compulsory, even though no gym was available. Some children had their own, but most of us used the ones provided by the school. The school stored them in an evil-smelling, dank cupboard, and we fought to get a pair that almost fitted before each session. Known as pumps, daps or sandshoes, whatever you called them, they looked the same. Across the country, children ran around in rubber-soled, black canvass pumps, with the toes protected with a worn and flapping rubber cover and broken knotted laces.

There were no showers then after the gym lessons, don't forget we never even had flush toilets. No wonder the classrooms in those days had a distinctive aroma.

5

Skeletons in the Cupboard

Life jogged along quietly with very few changes through the early nineteen fifties. Our small school only had two classrooms and two teachers. Hence, I moved up a class and stood each morning at an assembly in front of a large map coloured mainly in pink to show the extent of the British Empire. Unbeknown to me this was slowly fracturing until we could no longer say that 'The sun never sets on the British Empire.'

Each day I joined the tiny assembly to sing a hymn with the rest of the class. We rarely knew what the words meant. I sang about a green hill far away without a city wall and wondered why a hill would need a wall, anyway. We ploughed the fields and scattered, knowing it was a waste of time at this time of the year, should have sown them three months ago. We prayed for those in trouble on the sea, and half the class had never seen the ocean, not in real life and certainly not on television, come to that none of us had seen a television. All the pictures of the sea in our books showed a flat blue expanse lapping gently onto a golden beach inhabited by a pair of laughing, immaculate children with buckets and spades.

At least I knew what the sea could be like. My mother had a younger brother, he had served during the war with the Royal Marines and was now a physical training instructor at a Commando training depot. A couple of times a year we would hear the throb of a powerful motorbike, and then Uncle Charlie would storm in, whirl my mother off her feet and throw me in the air like a rag doll.

He would open his kit bag and produce something for us all, a treat in silk for my mother, a bottle for my father and a toy for me. He also brought photographs and illustrations of battleships and aircraft carriers. He had a fund of stories, most of them funny. Still, as the evening drew on and the firelight cast flickering shadows across the faces of the friends who dropped in to share the entertainment, there would be an occasional glimpse of the reality of war. He served on the ship that sank the German Scharnhorst, and a shadow would cross his face as he told how many of her crew had perished in the freezing sea before their rescue. Out of nearly two thousand men, only thirty-six survived.

I took Uncle Charlie to Portsmouth where, unbelievably, over twenty of the hardy German survivors pulled from the icy sea many years earlier were attending a reunion. We walked into the hotel, and he was greeted by several old shipmates, now men in their eighties, some of whom he had not seen for over fifty years. They stood enthusiastically reminiscing, and a tall silver-haired man walked over and with a trace of an accent enquired 'Excuse me gentlemen, did any of you sink my ship?' As a Marine, my uncle had been part of the gun crew, and he nodded reluctantly. His ex - enemy extended his hand, and they exchanged a warm handshake, then his silver-haired adversary put his arm around my uncle's shoulders and said, 'I have a little gift for you'. He then produced a photograph he had taken of the British ship as it fired upon the doomed German battleship. Incredibly he had taken photographs until he was thrown into the water with the camera still around his neck and had kept the film until he could develop it. 'Not the Leica, the camera used to capture the image - British officer took it for safekeeping'.

It was an unforgettable evening with the old ex- enemies exchanging stories, drinking together as comrades, laughing and singing songs in both languages. As one of them said, 'We share the same enemy now, time.'

* * *

My mother's family came from Scotland and so his name, Charlie was always pronounced Chairlee; he was a stocky, balding figure, quick to laugh and quick to anger, popular with men and women alike and totally irrepressible. He was actually my mother's half-brother. The story would not raise many eyebrows these days, but over fifty years ago, it was still a scandal. My Great Grandfather was a miner and wishing to make a better life for himself joined the Army. He served in India and took part in Lord Roberts march from Kabul to Kandahar in 1882, a forced march of over three hundred miles through mountain terrain and crippling heat with a fierce fight at the end.

On the way home, he collected another medal at Khedive in Egypt for another march across burning sand and another fight. On his return, he was temporarily stationed on the Isle of Wight and here he met a young seamstress, described as a kiltmaker on the wedding certificate. Hence, presumably, there was no shortage of Scottish soldiers on the island. Having wooed and won her, they returned to Scotland and settled down to raise a family. Perhaps she would have had second thoughts if she knew what lay ahead, probably not. They lived in a single-story two bedroomed stone cottage in Cambusbarron, and here the little kiltmaker reared twelve girls and one boy.

I have a photograph of my Great Grandfather. He stares sternly from it. He has dressed in uniform again because he volunteered for service during the first world war. He was too old for active service though and spent the war guarding London docks, across his chest is a row of medals spanning campaigns covering nearly forty years. According to his obituary, he was an elder of the church and a founder member of the local temperance movement.

I also have a photograph of the entire family, and my Grandmother is a strikingly pretty girl of about seventeen. I don't know the circumstances. Perhaps she was just a rebel. She was married young to a local boy who was called up to fight in the first world war, my mother was born and her father's regiment, the Black Watch was sent to Egypt to fight. In a story as old as time, my Grandmother met a dashing merchant navy sailor, and they ran away together, Uncle Chairlee was the result.

The sailor sailed away as they often did, and my Grandmother returned home with my mother and her half-brother in her arms. There is a sad sequel to this familiar story. Many years later, the family found a cache of letters sent to my Grandmother by her sailor suitor. My Great Grandmother had concealed them, hoping against hope that her daughter would be reconciled with her husband, it was not to be, and eventually, the sailor, who was heartbroken at not receiving a reply stopped writing.

There was no doubt that my Grandmother was a pretty girl and even with the disadvantage of two children with two different fathers and a failed marriage behind her she met and married Sandy Black, the man who I called Grandad. He was a character, some would describe this as a euphemism for a reprobate, but he struggled to bring up my mother and Chairlee as best as he could. By the time my Uncle had left school at fourteen, he was a handful. One day he had committed some offence that he knew would result in good hiding from his stepdad and waited patiently until he heard the 'old man' coming. Chairlee leant over the railings and cracked Grandad across the head with the stick used for stirring the washing, then before he recovered he tied him up with the washing line, gagged him and bundled him into one of the outside privies. So far so good, then reality struck, he had not just postponed trouble he had quadrupled it.

Pausing only to grab the bit of money that he had saved from his job as butcher's boy Chairlee headed south. He didn't stop until he reached the south coast. Here he lied about his age and enlisted in the Royal Marines. War broke out, and he served in Norway, then on the Arctic convoys and collected a star for every theatre of war, including the far east where he was present for the signing of the treaty with Japan. Twelve years after leaving home, he strode up to his mother's door, a tanned, confident sergeant. The door flew open, and there stood Grandad. 'You're home then' said Grandad and followed the words with an uppercut that sent Uncle sprawling. Uncle Chairlee leapt to his feet, smiling, and his stepfather brushed him down and led him, unprotesting, to the pub for the first of what was to prove many sessions over the years.

6

Scraps

I was in bed with some childhood ailment; I don't remember what. But my parents were secure knowing that at last, they could afford for me to be ill as the Health service, with free treatment, had been up and running for over three years. Propped up in bed and given a pile of books and a radio to keep me amused, I revelled in my day off. This was the life! I thought of my classmates perched at their wooden desks, writing with scratchy pens dipped into inkwells filled with homemade lumpy ink. They would sit, tongues protruding between their lips in concentration. The paper was an economy issue and would be absorbent in places, shiny in others, and even had lumps of straw embedded in places to trap the unwary nib. I chuckled to myself as I imagined some of them in trouble for not producing neat work. An impossibility, given the materials we had to work with, but any complaint would receive the retort, 'A poor workman always blames his tools.' And the complainant would then face the inevitable punishment of staying in at dinner time and doing it all over again. Then circumstances changed, my Father's old employer died, and we moved home.

During the war, my father had served in the RAF on a bomber airfield in the fen district, and it was here that we returned. During the war, my parents had lodgings in a house attached to a grocer's shop in a small fenland town and had become friendly with the family. Auntie Gertie as I called her was in fact, my godmother. They were some of the nicest, friendliest, people that

I have ever met and treated me like one of the family, as did their daughter June who was about fourteen years older than me. Uncle Fred used to do his delivery rounds to the outlying, isolated homes in the fens in a horse and cart. Even the horse was friendly and used to hang his head over the stable half door and gaze at me with huge brown eyes until I pulled an old orange box over and climbed up on it to put my arms around his neck.

I loved visiting them, and they always made me welcome, and they also had a television set, a true novelty in those days. We could watch the Coronation, and packed with the older friends, relatives and neighbours seated on chairs and the children standing at the back, the room with the television was bursting at the seams. Afterwards, we had a meal which included tinned peaches and thinly sliced bread and butter. Surely life could not get much better than this?

I don't remember doing any lessons at my new school. Life was far too exciting, Sir Edmund Hillary climbed Everest, and we made massive models of the mountain, then there was the Kon Tiki expedition. We made models of rafts which disintegrated and sank in the river, and the Coronation was in the front of everyone's mind. We made a model of the coronation coach out of balsa. It had plasticine horses and wobbly wheels, but we were proud of it.

My parents then rented rooms with a young couple who were lucky enough to have a council house. It seemed luxurious to me with an indoor toilet, bathroom and running hot and cold water. I didn't gain a real taste for such luxuries, though, because we soon rented a cottage with no facilities. This didn't bother me; it was worth sacrificing the 'luxuries' to have a home that we did not share. Even if we did share a row of three brick-built outside privies, each with their own wooden seats with a hole cut in it and squares of newspaper hung on a rusting nail. Ventilation was more than adequate. There was a large gap at the top and bottom of the door and a decorative diamond hole cut in the door itself.

It was only a short terrace of cottages, so it was not too long a walk to the privy. Although, on a dark winter's night when the wind came whipping across from the surrounding fens, it felt long enough. None of the cottages had a garden. The front door opened onto the 'yard'. This was a short lane branching off the main road, and ours was Compass Yard, and only had cottages built along one side. Opposite to us was the side of a fish and chip shop and then a high brick wall. The terrace consisted of about six cottages. At the entrance from the main road, there was a chip shop on one side and a sweet and tobacconist on the other. At the bottom of the yard, beyond the brick privies and a standpipe for the water, was a paddock. We would climb the fence and walk through the long grass to the edge of a pond. I remember it as being large. There was a willow on the bank, old and gnarled with a hollow trunk smelling of damp and fungus, and we used to climb up inside.

Fishing in the pond for gudgeon, with homemade fishing tackle as we watched the coots and moorhens fussing about on the water, was a favourite. The birds became so used to us they would strut past on the bank within touching distance. It still amuses me to see a moorhen walk, with their feet several sizes too large for their bodies, and although they use them for swimming, nature has not provided web feet. Instead, each toe has an elliptical flap, and it looks as though the unfortunate bird has trodden in something nasty and is trying to shake it off as it walks.

Some evenings my friends and I called at the chip shop to see if there were any 'scraps.' These were the small pieces of batter that floated off the fish as it cooked and scooped out crisp and golden but largely unwanted by the adults. It's hilarious to consider that these are now available in Marks and Spencer's food hall as a delicacy when so many fish and chip shops north of Watford have given them away for years. Standing on tiptoe, we hopefully offered a penny for some scraps, and the owner usually rewarded us with a generous scoop, plonked onto a sheet of newspaper. We smothered these with salt and vinegar, and if we were fortunate, a few chips had sneaked onto the paper, and our proffered penny refused with a conspiratorial smile. In the dusk of a summer evening, there were always bats circling at the entrance to the yard, and we tossed a scrap or two into the air to watch the aerobatics as a bat would wheel and swoop onto the airborne scrap before rejecting it, jinking away into the gloom.

One evening I flicked a chip in the air and instead of being seized by a misguided bat, it caught the patrolling local policeman in the eye. He gave chase, roaring as the salt and vinegar worked its way into his eyeball. Luckily, we had the advantage of youth and escaped up the yard and into the paddock. Not that he would have charged us with anything, but it saved us a thick ear.

It was only a small town, and we roamed everywhere free of restrictions. Sometimes I would go round to see 'Uncle' Fred and 'Auntie Gertie,' and I would 'help' Uncle Fred as he loaded up the cart with the groceries, candles and paraffin oil for the deliveries. He also convinced me that the hundreds of snapdragons that grew around the garden need feeding with a minute piece of soil. I would go round gently squeezing the flower until the 'jaws' opened, allowing me to pop in a morsel. He would reward me with a sweet, as he solemnly thanked me. They were the first people I knew who had a television set, there was very little daytime television then, and the only programme I can really remember was Muffin the Mule.

June, their daughter, was courting and Derek, her fiancée, would arrive by bicycle. He was always cheerful with eyes that crinkled into laughter, and he had infinite patience with me and encouraged my interest in aircraft. He was in the Royal Observer Corps and on the evening when they met would sometimes arrive in uniform. June and Auntie Gertie always spoilt me, and so it was like having a second family.

Just outside the town, within easy walking distance, was the airfield where my father had served for part of the war. It was now being used for training and most days and some evenings the air would reverberate as a flight or two of four-engine Lincoln bombers would roar overhead, looking almost identical to their Lancaster ancestors. Life in the early nineteen fifties echoed much of the wartime era with rationing and shortages. Men in uniform with kitbags and rifles over their shoulders sat, patiently sipping tea, in every railway station waiting for a train to some obscure place that they had never heard of before. So, although there may have been less chance of being shot at on arrival at their new posting, the cold war with Russia was beginning and painting the coal heaps white was a vital part of survival.

As children we were vaguely aware of Atomic energy, I knew that an atom was a minute particle and that splitting the atom was a way of releasing vast energy. This seemed almost too easy to be true and in fact, try as we could, we never achieved it. First, we would take a brick and smash a piece off with a hammer. Then we pounded the fragment into dust. Finally, fine powder was left. 'What do you reckon?' I asked my friends. The knowledgeable ones shook their heads, gravely sucked their breath through clenched teeth and separated a couple of grains from the heap. There was now an air of tension. The timider retreated to a safe distance and covered their ears with their hands, and the sceptical gathered closer. Even these winced as I brought the hammer down to split an atom or two. I remained frustrated. Frantically I beat at my little pile of atoms until they became so tiny, they stuck to the hammerhead, but try as I might splitting that final atom eluded me. There was one redeeming moment, the hammer caught a stone a glancing blow, and a spark arced gracefully through the air. We agreed that the atoms had become so small that this was the best result we were going to get, so we counted the experiment a partial success. You could even smell the 'atomic' energy released by the spark.

7

Big Game Hunting

We did not stay for long in the flat and friendly fens. Next stop was to be Scotland. We moved to Kirkcudbrightshire, an area of breathtaking beauty. Now we were really living in the country. Our cottage was about three miles from a small village and lay about a thousand feet above sea level. The village itself dipped one toe in the sea and then straggled along the banks of a burn which widened slightly before meandering into the estuary and bay. The bay looked, for all the world, like a bite taken from a biscuit, with a small island like a left-over crumb in the centre. At low tide, the sea retreated leaving the mudflats stretching out toward the island, and the burn snaked out to reach it, leaving a deep channel.

The school lay at the far end of the village on a small hill overlooking the bay, and it was possible to stand in the playground and look out over the Solway Firth. I had acquired a bicycle, and the ride to school was exhilarating. I had a short distance to pedal and then once on the narrow tarmac road gravity did the rest and I sailed down the mountainside, dropping a thousand feet in three miles without touching the pedals. I had to pay for this coming home where three-quarters of the way I needed to push the bike. And the rest of the journey I conquered by standing up on the groaning pedals and wobbling up at just over walking speed.

The small village school was remarkably similar in looks to its English counterpart, even down to the coke-fired stove where we gratefully hung our wet clothes to dry out. The major difference was in the lessons, no model making and creative 'time-wasting' in this school. I was there to learn, and I wasn't to forget it. In case tempted to forget, a leather strap called a tawse hung on a brass hook on the side of the teacher's desk. I am surprised that it didn't wear out. For the slightest misdemeanour, or even for a spelling mistake or incorrect answer, some child, boy or girl, would receive a stinging lash on an outstretched palm from the thick, two-inch-wide tawse with the end divided by a series of cuts. Strangely enough, I was happy at the school, and despite being the only pupil with an English accent, did not experience any bullying.

The wild-life was outstanding, and waders covered the mudflats, and I have never seen so many oystercatchers in one place. The haunting sound of curlews accompanied my ride to school and my struggle home. In the winter great skeins of geese would swoop in, honking amiably to each other. We lived on a plateau about a thousand feet up the mountain where the burn paused in its headlong tumble to meander through an undulating meadow. It broadened out here and was only a matter of inches deep but still icy cold, clear and sparkling. The chickens were free to scratch around the meadow, and a small flock of guinea fowl accompanied them. The guinea fowl fussed around with their spotted feathers, catching the light, making them look quite exotic. At night they roosted in the surrounding trees and made excellent guards, complaining at the top of their strident voices.

I ate guinea fowl eggs. The first time was a shock, as the eggs are smaller than a hen's egg and rounder, so they sink down in the egg cup uncooperatively. Although it presents a smaller target, the novice guinea-egg-eater can still confidently and casually take a sideways swipe at the protruding egg. With a chink, the knife flies off at an angle, and when repeated several times, each blow is likely to become more vicious than the last. Eventually, the would-be egg eater gives up and tries to beat their way in from the top. However, the shell is very thick, and it is like trying to beat your way through a golf ball. It must be one of the few breakfasts where it is possible to use more calories, unwrapping it than consuming. It is worthwhile though; the taste of the egg is superb.

The meadow sloped gently back towards the belt of trees, separating it from the mountainside behind, and rabbits covered this southern facing slope in the morning and evening. Determined to catch one of these, I constructed a cage made from chicken wire on a wooden frame, with a door that dropped at the back. The door, held up by a piece of wood, had a notch carved into it. I slotted a sort of pendulum into this notch and hung a juicy carrot from the end, and the slightest touch on the pendulum brought the door crashing down. For weeks I inspected this trap, and each day my confidence decreased until I lost interest and gave up. Many years later, I mentioned to my father it surprised me I had caught no rabbits. "Oh, but you did, probably half a dozen" he replied, "I used to go out in the morning and let them go!"

I was about ten years old and roamed freely, the only proviso being that if I went up the mountain to the summit about five hundred feet above our home, I was to leave a note saying where I was going and carry a whistle for me to summon help. I could not come to much harm, but if I fell and broke an ankle, for example, it should be easier to find me. I was the only child for miles around, but I don't recall feeling lonely. I read a lot of books about big game hunters in Africa and India and must have looked a strange sight as I walked around with an air pistol and sheath knife strapped to my belt and a pair of binoculars slung around my neck. The occasional shepherd or keeper who I met on my safaris would nod or pass the time of day but never commented on my appearance, until one day when a genial, burly keeper stopped me. 'Do you like shooting laddie?', I nodded, although truth to tell I had shot nothing, but the odd tin can.

'I'll hae a word wi' your father. You could come on a fox shoot mebbe.' He was as good as his word, and a couple of weeks later I was sent down to his cottage, where his wife greeted me with a plate of scones, a jar of homemade raspberry jam and a glass of lemonade. Angus, the keeper, produced a little single-barrelled .410 shotgun and spent the next hour, or so, showing me how to carry it safely and observe all the safety rules. At last, I could fire it, and Angus let me shoot at the door of the old outhouse and patiently explained how the shot spread out and formed a circular pattern. I cycled home in a daze; I had joined the ranks of the big game hunters.

After a couple more training sessions, we had reached the stage where Angus would hide behind the shed and bowl a tin plate down the path. After I hit it three times in a row, he nodded in approval and proclaimed me good enough to go fox shooting. I should explain, there is very little fox hunting in Scotland, the control of foxes is not a sport but a necessary part of vermin control. I was almost shaking with excitement when the day finally came that I joined the motley shooting party. I was the only boy there, and most of the men greeted me warmly and offered words of advice. 'This your fust time then?' I confirmed it.

'Well, let me tell you, yon fox is no' like the wee English creature, see, the hill fox is a braw, muckle beast.'

They described a fearsome animal, the terror of the mountain. Why the only reason that the wolves had moved out was their fear of the ferocious fox. I felt less confident, by the time I was positioned at the foot of a track leading into the plantation in a lonely, gloomy glen. All my confidence had evaporated, and I stood, gripping my gun with staring eyes fixed on the track wending its way through the bracken. A thick clammy fog limited my vision to a few yards and muffled the sound, leading to a sense of isolation. The moisture clung to my woolly jumper, and the beads stuck to the fibres, giving the impression of mouldy cheese.

After an eternity, I heard the calls of the men driving the foxes down and the clacks of their sticks as they beat them against the trees to add noise. This was it then, I swallowed nervously and prepared to sell my life as dearly as possible. What if there were over one of the bloodthirsty beasts? I only had one barrel and would have to reload. Then I saw a russet flash and a small animal shot passed me and vanished into the heather, but I never saw one of the mighty foxes.

Angus came over 'Why did you no' shoot yon fox?' he enquired.

'Fox? What fox?' I asked, 'I only saw a weasel'. He rocked with laughter. All my fellow sportsmen laughed until they wiped tears from their eyes. Then they explained that most hill foxes were about half the size of their well-fed

English cousins. Even I saw the funny side of it. They explained the same trick caught most of them when they were young, and not all had stood their ground, but had run off to safety. They now accepted me as a fully paid-up member of sporting society.

Despite the lack of companions of my own age, I enjoyed living here, and the ride to and from school was also enjoyable most of the time. Once I turned off what passed for the main road and began the climb up to where we lived, it was rare to meet another person. There was just one part that I did not enjoy, particularly when it was getting dusk or when the mist would swirl in from the sea, wrapping me in grey cold tentacles. A few hundred yards from the main road there was a plateau with three old pine trees on a grassy knoll. The story was that in the last century a small farmhouse had stood here and so many supernatural events had occurred that a priest had attempted to exorcise it. Even he was chased off by the poltergeist, or whatever persecuted the farmer. Shortly after this, the family moved, and the place slowly fell into ruin until nothing remained but the grassy mound. I did not know the story at this time, but I always felt uneasy. There was something creepy about this spot, and I used to stand on my pedals and attempt to pass it as quickly as possible.

One evening I realised my worst fears as I heard unearthly feet behind me. I strained even harder, as I sought to gain speed up the rapidly increasing slope. It was no use. A powerful force knocked me off my bike, and I opened terrified eyes to see the flaring nostrils and curled, sweeping horns of the monster that stood over me with hate in its eyes. I looked at my bike lying on its side with the buckled back wheel still spinning where a sheep had butted it from under me. But the rage in the sheep's eyes was nothing to mine. Hurling my damaged bike at the poor animal I chased it down the hill, taking swipes with my satchel at its woolly backside. The lamb it was protecting outpaced us both.

An old fox understands the trap - Anonymous.

8

Sweeties and Treacle

We were soon on the move again, this time further up Scotland to live with my Grandparents in Cambusbarron, just outside Stirling. Now I was surrounded by children my own age, and a high proportion of them was related to me. My Grandmother was one of thirteen, and a lot of the family still lived in the village, cousins surrounded me, and I now had a relative in virtually every road round about.

My grandparents had moved from the old apartment block where my uncle had tied up his stepfather before leaving home to join the Marines. They now lived in a brand-new council house, no longer did the washing have to be done in a central washhouse. There was no joining a queue for the outside toilet; we did not have to share anything! There was even hot running water from a tap. It was too late for poor old Gran; they confined her to bed. She had severe arthritis, but worse than this, she had to have a leg amputated. Unbelievably there had been a terrible mistake, and they removed the wrong leg, taking away the only good limb that she had. I imagine that she would get compensation now, but she didn't get a penny then. However, it did not seem to bother her too much. She sat propped up in bed with her twisted old fingers painfully knitting away. Now and then, she looked out the window and smiled as yet another relative bustled up to the door. 'Just for a wee chat, and I've brought a little something. Shall I maybe pop the kettle on?' She had eleven sisters and a brother, so relatives were much commoner than money.

I admired my grandad. He was a short, stocky man who always wore a cloth cap, well maybe he took it off in bed, but I never saw him without it. He smoked a pipe and had a spare in the top pocket of his jacket. A few times he put the still-hot pipe in his pocket and lit up another. The smoke from his singeing pocket would join the smoke that whirled around him.

The first thing he would do in the morning was to make a cup of tea and light his pipe. His favourite breakfast was kippers, and his neatest trick was eating kippers, drinking tea, and smoking a pipe at the same time. It was an art form. Without pausing, he would spit out any stray bones, puff out smoke and slurp tea. His little terrier sat quivering with anticipation until it had the skin from the kippers neatly piled on the lino in front of him, which the little dog licked as clean as a whistle.

One day two of my cousins, and I sneaked a pipe and tobacco, and we sat on the fence at the back of the houses, passing the pipeful of tobacco up and down the line. We got it drawing enough to take a few mouthfuls each, what an experience, after the second puff the world span round and I toppled gently off the fence to lie in a nauseous heap. My green-faced cousins joined me very shortly! This confirmed my opinion of the old boy. He was an invincible superhero; he could smoke this and eat kippers.

In fact, he was a real character, and every time his name comes up, I hear another story about him. He had quietened down by this time, although I do recall him cycling around with a hammer and chisel and pot of red paint carefully converting the ER-II into ER-I on post boxes. 'I've nothing agin' the wee lass, but she's only the first Elizabeth of Scotland ye ken.'

He had earned a precarious living as a dealer and carrier, with his bread and butter, such as it was, coming from a small coal round. On a Monday morning he would set off with a few shillings given to him by my Grandmother, and on a Friday, she would wait at the door for him to return and hand back a little more than she had given him.

This was not always the case. Sometimes she waited in vain until the pubs shut, and he came rolling home puffing whisky fumes through his whiskers, having spent the small profit on drink. Granny was resigned to this by now, but back in the days when she had two good legs and a fearsome temper, there were rows that the neighbours still spoke of in hushed tones. One particular time after two weeks of little or no money he arrived home to great her with the words, 'They'll be no money this week, woman.' He swept his arm behind him and pointed proudly to a gleaming cart pulled by a fine, sleek horse that stood outside. 'I bought yon beast and cart down the pub. It's making do you must be this week.'

With a screech that could be heard the length of the Forth granny grabbed a felling axe that leant against the woodpile and wielding it about her head attacked the shiny cart reducing it to firewood and causing the terrified horse to bolt in one direction and granddad in another. I never saw the horse again. Legend said that it dived into the Irish sea and swam home, but it is more likely that the tinkers who sold it to Granddad had recovered it gratefully. I saw the old boy after he exhausted his credit in the pub, he returned cap literally in hand and scraped up enough money to buy another horse and cart. This time a knocked kneed old nag pulling a battered cart with one wheel that tilted inwards and another that wobbled erratically.

By the time that I was living with them, Grandad drank solely at the weekends, and my grandmother and teetotal Auntie even frowned upon this. He would be locked out of the house to spend the night sitting in the porch. This seemed to neither do him lasting harm nor discourage him, in fact to the contrary. He would brush the frost off his moustache and shuffle off to the pub for a 'warmer'. However, I felt sorry for him and would sneak down the stairs to let him in. He would reward me by bringing me back a miniature bottle of rum. Inevitably, we were both caught and dragged in front of my grandmother. "What day ye think you're dain' giving the wee lad rum?"

"Well" my Grandad replied "He's too young for whisky ye ken"

* * *

If you go to Stirling now, you will see a real tourist area. The ancient castle dominates and rises from the plain and proudly lords it in splendour over the surrounding green countryside. Standing on the rocks that rise from the plain, it overlooks the Forth, sparkling as it makes its serpentine sweeps and curves towards Edinburgh. No doubt it was like this for many centuries, previously. The countryside green and peaceful, except for when English armies fought and lost in the fields around.

In the mid-fifties, things were different. Then coal was a major industry, and slag heaps were common. The stone quarry was running at full production too, just at the back of our council estate. Now and then there was a dull boom, and the ground would shake, rattling plates on the shelf. I loved it. We were still free to roam everywhere, and there was open countryside all around. I had a cousin who lived about two miles away. I would make my way down a minor road and then turn off up a track which led into a wood. About half a mile up the trail was an old brick-built bungalow where she lived. In fact, it was the back way into a large country estate, and this was one of the old gardener's cottages. My uncle had bought it for the proverbial song when the estate broke up, and he had also purchased the old walled kitchen garden.

A substantial burn rippled down beside the track, and it was well stocked with trout. The woods were populated with game, and rabbits bobbed about the grassy banks. Uncle Bob ran it as a smallholding and also kept a few pigs. Sweets were still difficult to come by, even more so when you did not have any money. And we hit on a brilliant idea. The meal that we fed the pigs on contained molasses and these blackened shrivelled lumps looked a little like dried banana skins or dates. It may sound repulsive, but they were as delicious and as sweet as syrup. We went through every sack and sorted them out, laying our treasure to one side. Not only did we eat them, but we also now had currency to exchange for other goodies. However, I suspect that our customers would have been horrified to know that they were eating a dinner stolen off a pig.

The burn that tinkled alongside the track down to the smallholding was big and swift enough to run a mill. The mill was no longer in use, but the ancient water wheel still revolved slowly. Half of it sat below ground in the stone-built, moss-lined sluice and the other half above ground - they built it of wood, and it was very similar to a larger version of the wheels found in hamster cages. Like hamsters, we delighted in jumping inside and running around as the wheel revolved. Unlike hamsters, we were not in control of the speed. The flowing water dictated that, of course. Perhaps the wheel was turning a little faster one day. Maybe I was a little clumsier or slower. I wormed my way out from behind the wheel onto the bank, and one of the wooden spokes clamped down onto my leg, leaving me flat on my back with my legs dangling inside the wheel.

Nancy, my quick-thinking cousin, forced a tree bough under the spoke, but could not turn the wheel back against the pressure of the water. But it took a lot of pressure and saved me from a broken leg, or worse, as the water pressure built up. I lay trapped like an animal in a gin trap until help arrived, at which point they shut down the sluice gate, turning the wheel backwards and pulling me to safety. There was nothing broken, but I could not walk, and they decided doctor ought to look at me. But this posed a problem. There was no telephone, and the nearest one was in the village, there was no car. The ancient horse was the other side of the woods and had never moved above walking speed in his life. By the time he'd backed protesting into the shafts of the cart, I could have crawled the two-and-a-half miles to the village. The solution was simple. I sat in an old wooden wheelbarrow with an iron wheel, and they pushed me down the bumpy track and along the lane to the village.

News travels fast. For the last part of the journey, cheers from onlookers encouraged us, as we made our triumphant entry and we trundled to a stop outside the cottage with a brass surgery sign screwed to the stone wall. This was way before the day's surgeries became 'efficient' and appointments were needed, so immediate treatment was available. I did not get out of the barrow before the younger of the two doctors appeared. He couldn't have been more than sixty, and he bustled out with his inevitable black bag and dangling stethoscope. He prodded and bent my leg, making the non-committal 'mmh' noises that experts are so good at before straightening his back and looking my uncle in the eye. 'Poor wee man. You'll need something quickly' he said. I nodded, but the doctor ignored me and led Uncle inside from where he emerged sometime later glowing gently and smelling of the best malt whisky. I was carried into the back kitchen and given bread and black treacle sandwiches by the Doctor's wife until Nancy arrived. She sat me on the saddle of an old bicycle before pushing me home because I could not turn the pedals. I could walk, albeit with some pain, within two or three days. I still regard water wheels with caution, and on the whole, believe that malt whisky is a better remedy than bread and black treacle.

9

Drama and Conflict

By the time I was twelve we had moved back to England, first to Bedfordshire and then on to Suffolk. At least I was getting an excellent education in British geography and went to eleven different schools. We were to settle in Suffolk for some time, and I went to the same school for two years, this shows how short a time I spent in some others, there was hardly time to carve my name in the desk lids of most of them.

This time I was fortunate. The school that I went to was just built and was a perfect example of what they meant a Secondary Modern school to be. After the schools I was used to, it was light, airy and had a relaxed atmosphere. The staff was mainly young and enthusiastic, and I do not recall the slightest problem with discipline. We were all used to a strict regime, but the atmosphere at this school was much friendlier, and we had no wish to spoil the easy relationship that existed here. We knew that there was no expectation of passing any exams, O'Level's existed, but only the grammar school pupils entered, and we left school at fifteen, a year before they took the exam. This meant that there was no pressure. We enjoyed a full range of activities with a lot of emphases placed on vocational subjects, and high standards in metalwork, woodwork, and horticulture, these being the likely way for most of us to earn a living.

Although I can't claim to have worked hard, I enjoyed all subjects except for maths. I was content to let the subject drift over my head and enjoy the view from the large fashionable windows, particularly if the girls' netball team was playing at the time. Built on a greenfield site, gardening lessons involved a lot of double digging to improve the soil. No doubt this is a lost art to modern schoolboys, I say boys because the girls could not take part then. It was assumed that in later life, boys would produce vegetables and the girls would be in the kitchen turning them into nutritious meals.

Double digging involved digging a trench and filling it with manure - I can just hear all the Health and Safety gurus tutting away and muttering about manual handling, substances hazardous to health and other fears yet to be invented. The only hazard was me. My over-enthusiastic digging harpooned the boy working next to me as I nailed his wellington to his foot, and his foot to the floor, with my well-worn fork.

When I subsequently broke a spade, leaving the blade stuck in the ground and the jagged handle in my neighbour's thigh, they forbade me to work in a group. After this, they condemned me to wheel heavy barrow-loads around at a safe distance or break up stones for hardcore, a sort of one boy chain gang. This I really enjoyed. I did not receive any punishment, nor did an irate parent arrive seeking compensation, accidents were accidents then.

One of my favourite subjects was English, Mr Brazil the teacher also ran the school drama club, and I became an enthusiastic member, admittedly because the initial attraction was that of being outnumbered four to one by girls. There was a lot more flexibility then, and a lack of a syllabus, so teachers from other departments joined in with the art, woodwork and sewing departments making scenery, costumes, and props. Metalwork class came up with a lot of ingenious devices, including a machine to imitate the sound of the wind. This consisted of four spiral curtain wires, (normally stretched between two hooks and used to support net curtains) fastened to a disc. They attached this to a hand-operated grinding machine that was previously used to sharpen chisels. We found a small boy to turn the handle. As the speed increased, the noise would build to a howling crescendo. Unfortunately, when the speed dropped the wires snaked about, and the peace after the storm was often punctuated by a yelp as the operator was flicked across the thigh or had a small chunk of ear removed. There was also the danger of an unwary passerby being flailed, but despite these minor design faults, the wind machine was so popular that we used it in most productions and wrote it into the script where possible.

A generation of audiences must have confused The Tempest with Midsummer Night's Dream and also wondered why an invitation to play tennis was issued in the face of a howling gale. Fortunately, there was no shortage of willing first years to turn the handle. They did not know of the sadistic tendencies of the machine, and their elders wore long trousers that hid the scars. There was an assembly every morning then for hymns and a prayer, and the headteacher seemed to find nothing strange in conducting this from a mock-up of Noah's ark or a facsimile of the Globe theatre.

In one production I played the part of Noah's black son, greasepaint was expensive and to save money was only used on my face. My arms, chest, shoulders, and legs were painted in black poster paint. The dress rehearsal took place with just my face blackened, and I did not appear in all my glory until the opening night dressed in a loincloth and impressively blackened. All went well for perhaps a quarter of an hour, and then the drying paint shrank. Small cracks appeared, these rapidly joined until I looked like a photograph of a drought-ridden mud hole. It was also unbearably itchy, and I could not resist a furtive scratch which made things worse. Most of the audience must have been convinced that my character was suffering from a virulent skin disease. Daphne, who played my stage wife disguised most of her horror but at the point where I was supposed to kiss her, drew back with a disgusted expression, and whispered "Don't you dare" under her breath. As a final indignity, I had to catch the bus home without having time for a shower, I pulled my normal clothes on over the top of my costume and sat scratching manically for the three miles home. The bus was packed, but I had both seats to myself. Passengers would see the empty seat and go to dive in, only to look at me and flinch away, pretending that they would really rather stand. People were looking at me and whispering behind their hand until I finally left the bus in a shower of black dandruff.

To make matters worse, we did not have any running hot water at home, so I had to stand in the garden and be washed down like a dog that has rolled in something nasty. After three nights of this, my character developed a real chip on his shoulder, and a generation of audiences are probably convinced that Ham, the son, was a sociopath, likely driven insane by an incurable, disfiguring skin condition.

* * *

My parents decided that they would try a new venture, and we moved into the nearby small market town of Bury St Edmunds. This is the first and last time that I have ever lived in a town, not that I minded, I still attended the same school, and my parents were now running a fish and chip shop. I would often get a lift home from school with one teacher who would come round to collect their taxi fare in the form of free fish and chips.

We also received free cinema tickets for advertising in the shop and visiting circuses and shows were also generous. We lived in a cottage attached to the shop, the shop itself had a flat roof, and it was possible to get out of a bedroom window and sit up there watching the world. It was a beautiful old town. There is a market square in the centre with roads leading off from opposite corners. One road leads down to the ancient Abbey ruins surrounded by tranquil gardens. When I lived there, a roller-skating rink stood in the square's corner. A museum sat in the opposite corner, and in between was a cinema. The town also boasted a dog track and an outside swimming pool. There was plenty to do. A slight drawback was the sugar beet factory on the edge of town. This meant that when the wind was in the wrong direction, the whole town was enveloped in a sweet-smelling fug.

East Anglia was studded with American Bases, and at the weekend the ancient town would be flooded with Americans. Personally, I always found them polite and considerate, prepared to hand the candy around, even after they discovered that I didn't have a sister. The trouble started when the Liverpool Regiment was posted nearby. Rumour had it that the Americans had accidentally bombed or shelled the regiment during the war, which had only ended ten years previously, and the Scousers had never forgiven them. I sat on the roof and watched a few pitched battles, most of which were broken up by the swift arrival of a jeep load of American Military Police. Parade smart and with pristine white steel helmets and guns strapped around their waists on immaculate webbing, the so-called 'snowdrops' would leap from the jeep and sharply apply their nightstick to the head of any combatant, without prejudice to nationality or rank.

This probably did not endear the 'Yanks' to the 'Scousers'. Still, nobody complained, and at least it provided a short term and spectacular solution to an increasing problem, an art that some would say the Americans have honed to near perfection even though our American Allies are now reduced to practising it on foreign countries.

10

Plucky Times

We were soon on the move again, and I was sad to leave behind the thatched cottages of East Anglia with their colour-washed walls. I was even sadder to leave Daphne, Molly, and Stella from the drama club and even more so the lovely Pat. Pat was a young Doris Day lookalike with whom I shared innocent trips to the cinema and walks through the tranquil Abbey gardens.

A move to Hampshire, to a green and peaceful valley where the river Test swept across its chalk bed to meet the Anton, was our destination. To my great delight, there were even more beamed, thatched cottages and the landscape was even more picturesque with wooded hills rolling gently down to the chalk streams. Whatever my father had been looking for must have been here because he was to spend the rest of his days in the area with no wish to move on.

I finished my schooling here with a few months at an all-boys' school. Built in the nineteen twenties, the attitudes and ethos had remained—solid red brick square unimaginative buildings and mostly teachers to match. Making the best of the situation, I coasted through lessons and reserved my energy for cross-country running and rugby, working where and when I could to save some money to buy a motorbike.

There was no shortage of opportunities to earn money then. None of the service industries existed; it must be hard for young people now to imagine a world without Macdonald's. But agriculture and horticulture were very labour intensive, and something always needed planting, weeding, harvesting, cutting, or hoeing. I plucked turkeys, carted bales, scythed thistles, and during wet days in the long summer holidays sat on a bale of straw in the old wooden barn. I perched on top its staddle stones and mended sacks while listening to the banter of the older men and the stories of conquests of yesteryear, with the occasional war story thrown in. Relaxing with their peers, the rich Hampshire accents would roll around the barn, much as they had done for centuries 'What's think you? Buggered if I b'aint a goin' t' thic ole pub ternight an'avin a skinful'.

'Do 'ee go thure 'ur 'ull skin 'ee, you'm puggled if you think 'er 'ull wear that.'

Which roughly translated for those without the benefit of a rural education means, ' I think I will go to the pub for a few pints tonight'.

'You must be mad. Your wife will be annoyed.'

The sack mending would take place sitting on straw bales with all the men smoking, either a hand-rolled cigarette or a pipe, in a wooden barn, packed with straw and festooned with cobwebs. This was sixty years ago and no doubt it had been like this for many years before, but I drive past the barn now, and there is no sign of a fire. No son or daughter of these men is employed here currently, mending sacks or otherwise. You will find them in their non- smoking, politically correct offices hunched over a computer devising risk assessments for changing light bulbs.

I have a few scars to show from those days, though we just learned to take more care. These were small penalties to pay for the privilege of enjoying a healthy, carefree existence and having the freedom to chug across fields in an ancient, rusting tractor that had to be literally fired into life with a cartridge. With the wind in my face as I bounced up and down on the metal seat, mounted on a spring to absorb most of the shock, and the steering wheel fighting my fourteen-year-old hands, I felt like a man. And unbelievably to me I was being paid for it. This beat being at school, roll on the next holiday.

We lacked many modern inventions and innovations—for instance, feminism and sexual harassment. Women tended to stay at home and scrubbed, washed, cleaned, and cooked. With no modern appliances to make life easier, fires to light and meals to prepare with no ready-made options and the need to catch the bus into town for the shopping, their life was difficult. By the time that they had fitted in a few baking sessions, darned a heap of socks, and heated the flat iron by the open range, their man would be home demanding more food.

By contrast, the breadwinner enjoyed total freedom. All he had to do was tumble out of bed and shiver around the house until he lit the fire. Then he usually washed and shaved at the kitchen sink, stropping his razor on the thick leather strop hanging from a hook while he waited for the kettle to sing on the range, signalling hot water for tea and shaving. By now it was getting late, probably six-thirty for a seven o'clock start, he was tumbling out the door. Grabbing his bicycle and with sandwiches and a bottle of cold tea, or if he was fortunate, a thermos flask stuffed into an old army haversack, he pedalled towards the factory hooter, builders yard or farm gate. Arriving before time, they would expect him to be working at seven. Not just arriving. At ten they would allow him a ten-minute break and then work for another three hours before a half-hour break to snatch a bite to eat. Some enlightened businesses would allow a ten-minute break in the afternoon. Usually, if the day were finishing at five, there would be no break, if the light permitted those working outside would carry on until six. I once heard the following conversation, 'Where do you think you're off to?'

'To the toilet Guv.'

'What again! That's twice today. You eat in your own time, don't you? Don't waste time getting rid of it in mine.'

So twelve hours after leaving home the breadwinner returned, all he had to do was get the coal in for the next day, chop some kindling wood, dig over a bit of garden for the vegetables, repair his work boots on the metal last and repair a puncture. As the politician said, we had never had it so good.

Actually, most men and women would not have swapped places, and each respected the other's contribution. Most working-class men were content to hand over their unopened wage packet each week, leaving their wives to deal with the finances and issue a bit of money for beer and baccy. No doubt there was deprivation in some areas, mainly the cities, I would imagine, but in the areas of full employment and rural districts life jogged on contentedly enough with brighter prospects in sight. The husband would eagerly read the Motor Cycle news each week, imagining how the coveted BSA or Matchless would mean trips out and more employment prospects, his wife would read Woman's Weekly and visualise life with a vacuum cleaner or fridge. Some brave pioneers even took out hire purchase and bought the treasured items. It only took a bit of overtime to pay for them on the 'never-never,' but unfortunately, this meant less time to enjoy the new acquisitions.

If you had a Hoover, why not buy a fitted carpet? After all, the Missus could get a part-time job to pay for it and with all the time saved she could do a few hours extra paid work, get a washing machine and save more time. Freedom for women was arriving. Eventually, they would become so free that all they needed to do was work full time to pay for all the labour-saving gadgets!

This was a few years into the future for me. We didn't even have a tap inside the kitchen, and it would have been pointless trying to fill a washing machine from our protesting, clanging pump.

It was the school Christmas holiday, and I was earning a bit of money by plucking turkeys. I was the youngest out of a group of perhaps ten, and we sat on benches in an old Nissen hut in two rows facing each other. There was the inevitable banter as we worked away, and now and then the farmer's young wife would bring in fresh birds and take away the freshly plucked carcasses. She was in her mid-twenties, a local beauty who had married a farmer's son and had been to school with most of the young men there. There were admiring glances at her tight jeans as they passed at eye level, and occasionally a hand would sneak out and pinch the denim. This resulted in a squeal and small jump followed by a playful slap to the cheek of her assailant. I watched this with interest, and after she had returned my smile, I plucked up my courage and ventured a furtive pinch. The reaction was not what I expected; she paused and then wiggled backwards on to my hand, looking down at me mockingly. Ten pairs of eyes watched expectantly. Confused, I dropped my hand, and a glow spread quickly across my face. A wave of laughter shook the corrugated metal walls as I frantically returned to feather plucking. Periodically throughout the evening the age-old refrain 'He wasn't a feather plucker, he was a feather plucker's son who sat there plucking pheasants 'till the pheasant pluckings done' would ring out and my discomfiture would be enjoyed again.

I still see her occasionally as she steps down from her son's Range Rover and passers-by probably wonder why the tweed-clad matron with the Margaret Thatcher hairstyle has a sudden twinkle in her eye.

* * *

Employment for youngsters used to be straightforward as less than five per cent of the population was expected to go on to university, mostly males. Most Grammar School students would stay on until they took their 'O' Level or 'A' level exams and then enter employment. The civil service had its own entrance exam, the armed forces were not looking for graduates, solicitors usually started as clerks, and many other professions had their own entry method for trainees.

For the rest of us, life was straightforward. At fifteen, you left school and started work. I did not know anyone my age who was not working. Most companies had apprenticeships for those who wanted to learn a trade and the opportunities were almost endless for a young person taking this route, many a managing director had started on the shop floor. It was common to continue education at night school and compulsory with most apprenticeships. Perhaps the majority took so-called 'dead-end jobs' in factories or semi-skilled occupations and had to content themselves with only earning as much as the teachers who had condemned their choice.

Getting a job was also simple, either your brother, sister or friend would let you know when their firm was 'taking on' people, or you would wheel your bike up to the door, knock and ask for a job. No one asked for qualifications; it was assumed that you didn't have any. If they liked the looks of you or were desperate, they would often agree to give you a trial and see how it worked out. By the time you were eighteen, you had been working for three years and probably knew your job well. Even some apprentices were being paid a full man's rate although they had a couple of years before their apprenticeships finished.

It was into this free and easy world of work that I was to enter. I had no expectations except to enjoy myself and earn enough money to buy a motorbike and was as pleased to be leaving school as they were delighted to be rid of me; I was not to be disappointed.

We were living on a farm about five miles from the small market town, and I either pedalled into town or caught the steam train that chuffed gently in, mainly following the course of the chalk stream through the water meadows and thatched villages strung out along its banks. These were the days before Beeching had used his remarkable foresight to close the rural railways, increasing the use of road transport and boosting the building of new roads. There used to be two stations in Andover then. One to serve the town centre, a few hundred yards away, and the other at the junction of the mainline to London, which still exists.

I was on the train to town one day and looked across the carriage at a sailor opposite to me whose luxurious set of whiskers puffed out and deflated as the snores echoed around the carriage. He sprawled out with his bell-bottomed trousers propped up on canvas kit bag. As the train shuddered into the station with a slight squeal from the brakes, he snuffled and snorted before settling down again. I hesitated, then just before stepping out onto the running board and down onto the platform, I shook him by the shoulder. Alarmed, he opened his eyes, read the station name and frantically scrabbled around, just shouldering his kit bag in time to leap out as the train jolted off again in a cloud of smoke and steam. He looked around blankly, 'Where am I?' I pointed at the station name. He had previously looked a benign bewhiskered figure. Now his face contorted from bewilderment to blind fury as he realised that he had got off at the wrong station and had now missed his connection. 'I wanted the Junction, you git' he roared as I rapidly beat a hasty retreat.

Happiness is the harvest of the quiet eye - Austin O'Malley

.

11

Moles

My father was a kind man. He was fond of animals with one exception, moles. He regarded each new freshly dug mound on his lawn as a personal affront and beat it flat with a spade, cursing under his breath. Eventually, he would snap, and the great vendetta would start. He tried borrowing mole traps and burying them in the runs, but either the moles no longer used that run, or they diverted around it and went off to bring a few friends back to see the latest attempt to catch them. He blasted lumps from the lawn with a shotgun whenever the wind caused the grass near a molehill to ripple. If this resulted in a deafened or traumatised mole it never showed, in fact, it seemed to encourage them.

The dog avoided the area, probably wisely, having calculated the chances of being beaten to death with a shovel or blasted into oblivion were extremely high. Sometimes Dad resorted to desperate methods. On one occasion he went muttering around the garden and carefully removed the little heaps of earth to expose the tunnels underneath. He followed by pouring petrol down each hole and then sprinkling it over and around the mouth of each tunnel. Confident that he had sealed the fate of his enemies, he retreated to a safe distance, lit a bundle of oil-soaked rags and threw it at the petrol-soaked runs. The result was disappointing. True, there was a satisfying whoomph, but it quickly settled down into flickering flames as the petrol-soaked earth acted as a giant wick. I think the moles preferred warm soil because they came back in force. He was undaunted but bowed out of the conflict while he devised a new strategy.

I really enjoyed a trip to the cycle store. On opening the door, a bell would tinkle and usher you into a veritable treasure house. First, there was the smell, a combination of rubber, oil, and leather from the saddles. Then there were rows of shiny new cycles, all black enamel and glistening chrome. Nearly every bike was black, massive frames that owed more to the designers of five-barred gates than anything else. The handlebars were chrome tubes that turned back at ninety degrees at each end, with complicated rods leading down from their flattened end to form a lever, and the design had not progressed since before the war. They were still objects of beauty to us.

We built our bikes out of discarded wrecks, and the paintwork was dull, and the chrome pitted with rust. If you were lucky, you would have a Sturmey Archer, three-speed hub giving a choice of low, medium, or high gears, and a lever mounted on the crossbar often operated this. This was a great disincentive to standing up on the pedals. A vindictive eunuch must have designed this. A guy who was waiting for another victim to slip and go sliding up the crossbar before the operating lever brought things to a screaming halt. Sometimes when we were out on our wrecks, we would hear a whirring and a hum of tyres and a group of racing cyclists would sweep past. So, we knew that drop handlebars and sophisticated gears existed and cable could operate that brake, but there were no such exotic machines here. There was one exception. A friend of mine called Ann in the next village had a pink bike with white-walled tyres and white handlebar grips. She was the prettiest girl in the village, and many a head would turn to watch her go by. I am almost certain that it was not the bike that was being admired, though.

There were no such bikes in the cycle store though, just ranks of solid working bikes. Festooned with tyres, the walls had shelves holding boxes of chains and all the impedimenta of cycling and the posters on the wall depicted apple-cheeked Edwardian maidens and their straw-hatted admirers about to set off on a cycle ride. I always felt that I could find a solid-tyred boneshaker tucked away in the ranks of bikes if I looked hard enough.

After threading through the forest of handlebars, you reached the oil-stained counter, and another world opened up. In glass-fronted cabinets were Webley air pistols and chained to the wall were the Diana, Webley and BSA air rifles. A request would send the proprietor scrabbling under the counter for airgun pellets, paper targets, fishing hooks, floats or sheath knives. You could probably have equipped a safari from this shop.

Many years ago, cars and then bicycles relied upon acetylene lights. The gas was formed by placing calcium carbide in a chamber at the bottom of the lamp and allowing drips of water to fall on it from a small reservoir. I doubt if there were many lights like this on the road, but it was possible to buy acetylene lanterns and carbide from some cycle shops. Supplied in a red cylindrical container, they looked like a giant tube of smarties. I know that some unscrupulous poachers used to get a screw-top beer bottle, fill it partway with small pebbles, and add carbide with a splash of water. The top was then screwed firmly down, and the bottle dropped off a bridge or into a likely pool. As the bottle sank, the gas would rapidly expand and blow the bottle to bits underwater. The result. One or two stunned trout floating to the surface. Who knows, perhaps the fishing tackle section supplied them? However, we bought two or three tubes of carbide from the cycle shop and took them home for the next stage of the great mole offensive.

My father carefully exposed each tunnel and spooned in a generous helping of carbide granules. These were almost black and resembled broken up charcoal. He added a dash of water and covered the hole with earth again. He repeated this until he'd dealt with every molehill. He then sat on a wooden seat under the apple tree with the shotgun on his knee and waited for the gas to drive the moles up for air. A couple of minutes passed, and nothing seemed to happen. So, he pulled out his tobacco tin and rolled up a cigarette. I still have the container, and it's a clever idea. There are two rollers built into the lid. They attach a flap of oilcloth-like material between the rollers. Placing tobacco on a cigarette paper between the rollers, as the lid closes, the rollers move up, and the cigarette pops out of a slot in the tin's top. Voila – couldn't be simpler!

On the day of the great failed mole massacre, my dad placed the cigarette between his lips and lit up. He then flicked the match into the damp grass…

the explosion blew clods of earth as high as the apple tree, and other smaller detonations followed until the devastated lawn resembled a scale model of the western front. The rooks in the elms took off and circled wildly around, narrowly avoiding midair collisions all shouting directions to each other at the same time. The heifers in the neighbouring field kicked their heels in the air and sped for the far end of the meadow, and our cat left home for two days. It always had a haunted look after that, though, and a dropped teaspoon would cause him to climb the curtains.

My father exhaled the cigarette smoke through his nostrils and rubbed his hands together with delight. 'Wasn't what I expected, but that'll sort the little beggars out,' he chortled. My mother was not so pleased. As she pointed out, he had done more damage than the moles had to the lawn, plus breaking a window and driving the cat into a nervous decline.

The moles came back before the grass grew on the battlefield, and this time we left them to their own devices. I am sure that if there is ever a nuclear holocaust, the mushroom cloud will drift away to reveal a perplexed but unharmed mole blinking in the wreckage.

12

Mistletoe and Wine

I am sure that it is true that winters were colder in the nineteen fifties and early 60s. I know that homes were not, as a rule, centrally heated, and insulation was a thing of the future, but freezing, crisp winters were the norm, usually accompanied by snow. Perhaps I was just more aware of this because a lot of my transport was my motorcycle. I don't think so; many car drivers resorted to snow chains for a few days each winter, certainly in the rural areas. The chains wrapped around the back tyres, on a sort of leather belt with massive brass buckles and the sets of chains crossed over the tyre at intervals of about a foot gave added grip on snow-covered roads.

Lying in bed in the morning in the gloom of a winter's dawn it was sometimes possible to tell if there had been overnight snow by listening to the milk float trundling slowly past with a soft rhythmic thumping of the chains on a snowy road. The snow chains caused the bottles to chink against their metal crates. If a sudden thaw happened or the chains came into contact with a tarmac road, the float would almost jump up and down and vibrate, and the bottles would be in danger of smashing.

Very few cars had any form of heating, and the occupants wrapped up warmly, the driver wearing a short coat to leave legs free, usually with gloves on and a suitable hat. Invariably cars had blankets for the passengers if they expected a journey of more than a few miles. Only the newest cars had heaters. I didn't know anyone who had such a luxury. Some vehicles had a primitive electrical heater for the windscreen. This took the form of a spiral wire element partly enclosed by a Bakelite shield which directed the heat onto the windscreen, rather like a one-bar electric fire. Stuck on the screen by a circular rubber suction disc at each end of the element, this worked reasonably well if the screen was merely frosty. But when the car started moving and the wind chill factor took hold, driving in conditions like freezing fog became a test of endurance. The driver would hunch over the wheel with his nose inches away from the rapidly shrinking clear patch.

Fortunately, there was no seat belt to restrict his movement. Eventually, the law of diminishing returns ensured that he was so close that his breath froze on the inside of the screen and with teeth chattering like castanets he would pull over and scrape a patch clear enough for the rudimentary heater to work. If I left the bar to the electric heater on, it was likely that the battery would flatten. If not left on long enough, the task became a challenge that would have baffled Hercules.

Ernie solved the problem quite simply by bolting a paraffin heater to the floor of his old car and arrived at his destination smelling like a disaster in an oil refinery with eyes looking as he had been peeling onions. This was in the days before M.O.T. tests, but strangely enough most of us worked out that it was not the best idea, anyway we preferred chattering teeth to streaming eyes.

Heating houses was not simple, either. I met no one who had double glazing, and they built many houses of brick walls with no cavity. Loft insulation was almost unheard of, and the wind whistled through gaps. Only the very rich had central heating, and most of the population relied on coal fires and paraffin heaters. You may have seen 1950s advertisements, where Mother and Father are seated, smiling contentedly in comfortable chairs by a flickering fire - he is contentedly puffing on his pipe. Slippered feet stretched out toward the flames. She is knitting and smiling at the mischievous kitten creeping up on the ball of wool. Son is playing on the hearthrug with a Meccano set, and Daughter is gently combing the golden tresses of her doll. A dog stretches out to enjoy the heat from the fire.

Now for a taste of reality. Most of the heat from the fire is going straight up the chimney, the only exception being when the wind changes and the room fills with smoke. Now and then the cheap coal that is smouldering in the grate will give a hiss and crack, spitting out a red-hot sliver to add to the burn marks on the home-made rag hearthrug. They draw armchairs up close to the fire and form a tight protective semi-circle in a futile attempt to keep warm. This leads to bare legs being scorched and mottled with the heat leading to chilblains. Meanwhile, the back of the occupants' necks is subjected to icy draughts whistling in through gaps in the woodwork. If a dog were allowed in at all, it would fight its way to the front and lie, scorching gently, until the occupants could stand the smell no longer and drove it away.

Like many other houses, we had thick curtains hung over the doors and the windows, we also had rolls of padded material at the bottom of each door, like big chintzy jam rolls. Sometimes these were made to resemble 'sausage dogs', and we pushed these tight against the crack at the bottom of the door to lie there faithfully guarding us against the icy blast. Getting out of the typical door took proper planning.

Underneath the 'lino' and over the bare wooden floor we laid sheets of newspaper. This helped to cut down the draught from the gaps in the floorboards, but when the wind blew from the wrong direction, it caused an interesting effect. The whole of the floor would ripple as the wind lifted the combined paper and 'lino' covering. It fluttered in a series of undulating waves, only a few millimetres high, a very disconcerting experience to have the floor flapping like a sail beneath your shivering feet.

There was also a heavy reliance on paraffin heaters. A strangely coloured, ancient pink van delivered our oil. A small shivering queue would form, stamping their feet to keep warm, the frozen snow crackling like eggshells underfoot, as they waited for their cans to fill from the tank on the van. Bert, the paraffin man shuffled to the back of the van. His oil-impregnated mittens would probably have burned like beacons, and they reeked, but this did not stop him using the back of them to wipe the dewdrops off his bulbous, blue-veined nose. I never saw him without a scruffy balaclava pulled down over his ears. This, with his oil-stained old army greatcoat, gave him the impression of being a relic from some long-forgotten war. Conversation was not his strong point. He would insert a battered metal funnel into the top of the can, open the brass tap in the tank and grunt with satisfaction if he spilt some on your clothes or shoes. His mission completed, he would chug off, slithering in the icy ruts, pausing only to light up a cigarette which he would dangle from his lower lip in an optimistic struggle to prevent his oil-impregnated mittens from overpowering the taste of his 'fag'. He was one of the few who did not roll his own cigarettes though, even he drew the line at paraffin impregnated cigarettes.

I never found out what he did in the summer. Rumour had it he sold ice creams. I can't imagine that there was much call for paraffin flavoured ices though.

There were two main types of paraffin heater. One was a metal chimney sitting on top of a tank full of oil. A knurled brass knob could be twisted to raise or lower the wick, and a small window allowed you to see the height of the flame. When the flame burned blue, a small amount of smell accompanied a small amount of heat. We considered this to be ideal. When the flame turned yellow or orange, the heat would reduce, and the stench made your eyes water. This was the norm, and any draught made matters worse. The second sort was more interesting. In this type, we filled a gallon of oil into a round glass bottle. There was a cap on top with a spring-loaded plunger. We would place this upside down with the outlet nozzle pointing downwards. The weight of the bottle would depress the plunger, allowing the gravity-fed oil to saturate the wick. This would be cautiously lit with a match and the smoking, flickering wick adjusted, a half-round chrome reflector like a big metal saucer reflected the heat from this. They were effective, as were incendiary bombs, and the heater we had was determined to show its potential. If we jolted it, the flames flared impressively, but it never beat the original chimney version for fumes.

So, there we were, huddled around a coal fire, Father with a heavy cardigan and woollen muffler, Mother with a blanket wrapped around her legs to prevent her legs from scorching and a hot water bottle clutched to her chest. Me in mittens building Meccano with my bare legs tucked under the protesting dog who was merrily scorching away. Now and then a lump of coal would spit and hurl a red-hot ember at the fireguard, and we would all jump, even the dog would raise an eyebrow.

Were we miserable? Strangely not, we classed ourselves as lucky; we had heat, and we had food. The really unlucky ones were those who had to choose whether to starve or freeze, and I knew families who burnt their skirting and architraves to keep warm and hoped to replace them in the summer before their landlord discovered it.

When we finally moved into the old farmhouse with its solid stone floors, front porch and huge kitchen heated with a solid fuel cooking range, we could not believe our luck. We could sit at the opposite side of the room and still be warm, and the floor no longer shifted like the dunes of the desert. The front room was a different matter, but we only used this for high days and holidays. It was nice and cool in the summer, and the farm allowed us enough logs to keep it cheerful on the rare occasions that we used it in the winter, such as Christmas.

* * *

Christmas was different in many ways. There were only two days holiday but the evenings of the Christmas period were also a time for celebrating, and friends and neighbours would call round, often bringing some home-cooked delicacy, to join in a game of cards or monopoly. This would destroy the spirit of Christmas as arguments broke out over the games. This tradition carried on for many a Christmas. My then-girlfriend upheld the tradition by becoming highly indignant when we were playing cards and using matches in place of money. My father 'paid' her with a used match leading to accusations of cheating.

There would not be much alcohol. In our house, they limited it to a crate of beer and two bottles of VP wine. One red and one amber, which were referred to as Port and Sherry. There would be plenty to eat, though. All of it homemade apart from a selection box of chocolate which formed part of my Christmas present each year. Usually, the rest of my presents would be homemade, or more likely hand knitted.

We decorated the house with paper chains and streamers, and each year a tree would mysteriously appear. Often the first we would know would open the door to find a Christmas tree blocking the porch. Nobody except Townies bought a tree, the woods were full of them, and someone always wanted to swap a tree for a couple of rabbits or the odd favour during the year.

We boys used to go out on our bicycles and collect holly from the hedgerows, and it never occurred to us that this belonged to someone. Sometimes a farmer would appear and check if we only had enough for ourselves, and we were not selling it for a profit. If satisfied, he usually gave a cheerful nod, wished us the compliments of the season and gave us strict instructions to keep an eye open for 'They dang gypsies' who would strip the trees bare.

Not everyone understood the unwritten rules. There was a fine old Georgian Vicarage at the end of the village with a row of elm trees, home to scores of wheeling, raucous rooks. Beside these was an old ill-kempt orchard, the gnarled boughs of which were covered in mistletoe. The old Vicar understood the ways of youths he would turn a blind eye to a bit of scrumping during the autumn and willingly contributed mistletoe to the eager village lads. Perhaps he realised that it was all good for business and could eventually lead to a new crop of weddings and Christenings. At any rate, he was a benevolent old boy, and much loved and respected by all.

When he retired, a middle-aged man, recently ordained, took his place, having spent most of his life in commerce. There was a change in attitude. Suddenly the mistletoe was for sale. We were outraged! Nobody had ever bought it before, as far as we were concerned it was hung on trees by a superior being to feed birds (and the appetites of hot-blooded youths!). Doubtless, the new vicar had a point, after all, it had, indirectly, been planted by his boss and the Church Fund would benefit from any monies raised but this was tradition being trampled underfoot.

It was an evening like a scene from a Christmas card, not a cloud in the sky and stars twinkling like overdone special effects in a pantomime. The cold was enough to make you catch your breath, and we breathed shallowly as we slowly approached the silhouetted avenue of trees and stealthily laid the bikes against the hedge. Every sound was magnified in the frosty night air and singing could be heard from the village pub punctuated by an occasional bark from an alert or neurotic dog. Cautiously, we slowly made our way to the darkened orchard. Almost silently apart from the gentle scrunching of frost-brittle grass underfoot, plumes of vapour arising from our breath and threatening to freeze in our nostrils, we reached the old trees. As I climbed the tree, frost crystals were shaken off and gently shimmered to the ground, twisting, and turning like a swarm of midges illuminated by the brilliant full moon. In a matter of moments, we cut off a couple of bunches of mistletoe and dropped to the ground.

No doubt the Vicar thought that we had not seen him, and the Verger creep up the opposite side of the hedge and make their way out onto the road. Probably it seemed like a good idea to him to let the air out of our bike tyres and wait for us to return after all gamekeepers had been doing this for years to foil poachers.

Shaking with silent laughter, we trotted in the opposite direction. We went around the back of the old coach house before running up to the pub and retrieving our own bicycles leaving a mystified Vicar fuming over the bikes that we had 'borrowed' from outside the pub earlier in the evening. For some time afterwards, we could hear the rightful owner berating the Vicar for losing his valve in the hedge. It was a setup, of course. We wanted the Vicar to know that we had fooled him. If the intention were to steal the berries, we would have picked a stormy night when a choir practice was being held. The Vicar was tipped off in advance. Even Big Joe, the pigman who was using unholy language to the Reverend, had his tyre valve firmly in his pocket.

We were not old enough to drink legally, but we smuggled a couple of pints of shandy out of the pub, and the sound of laughter rose by several decibels as the story went around about how the Vicar was hoodwinked.

The following year the Vicar held the ladder for us and generously donated a few free bunches of mistletoe to the village, his Christmas collection more than made up for it.

A village is a hive of glass, where nothing unobserved can pass - Charles Spurgeon.

13

All in a Day's Work

Having now turned the grand old age of fifteen, I was free to launch myself on the unsuspecting world of commerce. I imagine that the school was as pleased as I was. There was no such thing as work experience, although it was not unusual to find an employer who would 'try you for a week and see how we get on.' The first of these was at a printing works, and some thought I might be suitable to become a compositor. I gave it a fair trial. In fact, I stayed longer than I should. I started at eight a.m. on a Monday morning and left at ten a.m. on a Monday morning. Unfortunately, it was the same morning. I listened to the clatter of machines, watched the serious faces as their harassed owners struggled to meet the deadlines, and concluded that this life was not for me. I did not object to working. Even hard work! I worked on the farm and was quite happy to work on the harvest from seven in the morning to seven at night. I hated being closed in. The thought of the same routine every day until they gave me a clock and ushered me through the door to prune my roses made my blood run cold.

So, newly unemployed, I walked down the road with my packed sandwiches still unwrapped in my dinner bag when I came across my next venture. I stopped at the showroom of a dealer in Morris Austin and MG cars and looked at a gleaming new MG sports car when the salesman came out. I have no doubt he intended to throw me out. It soon became clear that I knew more about the car than he did - I spent nearly all my spare money on car and motorcycle magazines, which I read from cover to cover. While he had other interests such as the pub, and as I discovered later, the wife of the local baker. As our conversation progressed, I gradually eased my way further into the rear of the showroom and into the workshop behind. I don't really know how it happened, but in any event, I soon wore a brown boiler suit and crawled under a car. This became the pattern for the next year, and they actually paid me for it. The grand sum of one pound ten shillings a week. The novelty of working with the gleaming cars that I had previously only been able to admire on the pages of Autocar and Motorsport, partly compensated for being confined in a fume-filled building smelling as all garages did in those days - of engine oil, grease and exhausts.

My commute was marvellous, and I used to cycle into work most days; it was about five miles from home, and if the weather was terrible, I could catch a steam train as it gently followed the valley from home to town. The train, paused at a village on the way, crossing and re-crossing the river that flowed past thatched cottages, water meadows and farmhouses. The cycle ride was also enjoyable, although the road did not follow the valley and wound up and down the chalky downland through clumps of beech trees and passed hedges heavy with dog roses in the summer and blackberries in the autumn.

One day, I was helping the electrician. He was a rotund, gentle man, and I never knew his name because inevitably, all his workmates called him 'Sparky'. Sparky had served in the Fleet Air Arm during the war, mainly on aircraft carriers, but he did not look like anyone's idea of a sailor. Imagine a friendly walrus, one wearing glasses that did nothing to hide his twinkling eyes. Being on the large side, Sparky was leaning over an open bonnet of a Morris Minor while I crawled under the car with an air line to follow his instructions and blow some oil and dirt off a component. Sparky leant over the car a little further, and my arm holding the airline came up to meet him from beneath. As my arm squeezed past the oily engine, I accidentally pressed the trigger, and a jet of high-pressure air blew the glasses off the end of Sparky's nose. Automatically, he jerked upright, and the back of his bald head smacked into the raised bonnet. A metal rod held the bonnet open, with a bent metal rod that wedged between it and the car. Unfortunately, Sparky's frantic jerk dislodged this rod, dazing him in the process. Where his head hit the underside of the bonnet, he slumped down across the engine, resulting in the unsupported bonnet closing like a giant mousetrap, leaving his frantically kicking legs clear off the ground. His kneecaps tried to beat the chrome off the bumper.

My respect for Sparky went up in leaps and bounds - he could be quite athletic when he tried. When they pulled him out from under the bonnet, he sat purple in the face with a pair of bent glasses with shattered lenses perched on his bleeding nose. He was wearing a length of polishing cloth as a turban, and the hand not holding a blood-spattered handkerchief was clenched into a fist he waved at me. He did not stop for five minutes. He described me using every profanity that he had heard in every port from the arctic circle to the South Atlantic, and when he had run out of them, he embellished the old ones and made up new words. He made suggestions that were physically impossible and wished fates on me that condemned my ancestors and descendants to the lives of a very interesting, but highly uncomfortable eternity. No one had heard him raise his voice before.

A couple of months later, I was sent to bring down a drum of underseal. Although the garage looked modern from the front, it was a former coach house and blacksmith's forge and therefore built on several levels with old staircases connecting what had been the hayloft with the workshop below. Underseal came in five-gallon drums. It was a black gooey substance that looked terrible and smelled worse, similar to matured cats' urine. I rolled the drum up to the top of the steep wooden staircase and then had a brilliant thought. Instead of putting the drum on my shoulder and struggling downstairs with it, why not just open up the hatch in the floor, roll the drum over and drop it down to the next level? Sheer genius, I could not think why no one else had used this method. No sooner said than done, I shot the bolts back and dropped the drum through the hole. There was a moment's silence and then a sort of squelching thud followed by a blood-curdling scream.

Convinced that I had murdered someone, I hurtled down the wooden staircase, and a terrible sight met my eyes. The hatch was actually directly above the small domain of Sparky. An immaculate area with polished tools hung on racks and neat shelves of spare parts—a place for everything and everything in its place. The metal drum had dropped through the hatch and landed upright on the painted concrete floor. The momentum had compressed the drum to about half its normal height, causing the lid to fly off and the contents to erupt for all the world like a treacle filled, evil-smelling volcano. Underseal slowly oozed down the walls and dripped in thick blobs from the ceiling.

In trepidation, I looked at Sparky. He had been standing behind his workbench, from the waist down he was spotless. His overalls always pressed, his shoes shining. From the waist up he had a coating of tarry underseal. His face was black, and his hands dripped with smelly underseal as he stood vainly trying to polish off his newly acquired spectacles. This time he was speechless and reduced to spluttering and vague grunts. Amazingly enough, I still had a job the next day, although it was weeks before Sparky did more than growl at me. Even then, he used to look around nervously and take his glasses off whenever I was closer than about ten feet.

Eventually, it was decided that a new spray shop was required and with no respect for planning laws, the task would fall to the odd job man. He would build a concrete block extension on the back, and they sent me along to help him. We dug out the footings using pickaxes and shovels before concreting the foundations and building the block walls. At last, I was happy. I could hear the birds sing and feel the wind and rain on my face. I went home each night, having used up my excess energy and happily returned each morning a little less stiff each time. I made my mind up. I would not return to life inside four walls.

Sparky was marginally happier than I was about my decision.

14

Buzzards and Badgers

I lay on my back on the sun-warmed grass, idly watching a buzzard as it majestically sailed over. It hung in the sky and wheeled away with its wings straight and motionless, a perfect gliding machine riding a thermal along the ridge. This was the life, free from petty restrictions, surrounded by the rolling downlands where Hampshire met Berkshire and so far from the road that the noise of an occasional car failed to reach us.

True, I was not as free as the buzzard, this was only lunch break, and we had a brief half-hour, but work was no hardship. The building industry in 1958 was a free and easy affair. We did not understand health and safety or legislation. We only recognised a 'fair day's work for a fair day's pay,' and the older craftsmen were happy to pass on their skills. I raised myself on an elbow and looked around. It was a peaceful, if not bucolic, scene. Old Uncle sat puffing contentedly on a short pipe in the shade of a lilac that was just bursting into bloom. He certainly believed in the saying 'never cast a clout until May is out.' He wore an old, hairy, tweed jacket over his bib and brace overalls, a flat cap that must have dated from the 1930s and a muffler round his neck. His face was brown and wrinkled, not the lines of care, just character and laughter lines, and intense blue eyes twinkled merrily when he did not screw them up against sun or tobacco smoke. Sitting on a log was Dick, in his forties, his dark hair starting to thin out. He was also a true countryman and the son of a shepherd. He was a source of stories and a never-failing, good-humoured companion. Normally whistling away, he would occasionally burst into the refrain of a Canadian folk song that he learnt during the war from his brother-in-law. This contained the memorable line 'I have tears in my ears through lying on my back, in my sleep as I cried over you.' If they meant it to be sad, it had the opposite effect on us.

Ron sat rolling a cigarette. He was a source of irritation to the younger workers such as me; he was officious, a self-appointed foreman of every situation. 'Right! Stand aside I'll show you how it's done, no no not like this. Look like that' Unfortunately for him, the 'like that' frequently resulted in a disaster, we would not laugh, quaking with inner mirth, we would thank him and ask for a repeat performance. He would glare balefully at us but was never sure if we were 'taking the Mickey' or not and would stamp off with two bright spots of colour on his already florid cheeks. Poor Ron, we made his life miserable. His battered old bicycle suffered innumerable unexplained punctures. We would replace the cheese from his sandwiches with harmless, but tasteless, leaves from the hedge and he would sit scowling and growling threats against his wife and her sandwich-making skills. These were totally empty threats, as he was scared to death of her in reality.

I am ashamed to say that we tormented Ron, yet he would never learn. If we felt lazy, we remarked how difficult a task was, and he would be there. Pushing us to one side, tongue clicking impatiently, he would grab the tool from our hand and 'demonstrate' the opposite. We would complain about the weight of something, and the florid, impatient Ron would bustle up and show the perfect way of moving large objects into difficult situations. He would inevitably tear his clothes, trap his fingers, and strain his back, but we would simulate admiration and then collapse with laughter when he had gone.

Today we were repairing a brick and flint barn, built perhaps two or three hundred years previously in this remote valley where the two coombs rolled down to the unmade dirt road. Time had stood still in this valley. The first swallows were hawking around after flies. High in the sky, that was good. High in the sky meant pleasant weather. When the air pressure dropped, so would the insects, and low-flying swallows would be followed by rain or a summer storm.

We started work at half-past seven in the morning, and most of us agreed on a ten o'clock lunch break. It was welcome. I arrived in the yard each morning at seven. We lived about eleven miles away, and breakfast grabbed at about half-past five in the morning was a distant memory. We stopped again at one for another half-hour, for what we called dinner and had a tea-break at three in the afternoon. Sometimes in the summer, we would work until six in the evening, and I would arrive home at about seven-thirty p.m., ready to eat enough for three grown men. I earned the princely sum of two pounds a week which was good. It was also about ten shillings (50p) above the true apprentice rate.

As soon as I was sixteen I bought a motorcycle, it was thirty-years-old. Mine had 'girder forks' - these were strange welded tubes with a central spring that absorbed some shocks from the road and no rear suspension, resulting in eye-watering jolts to the back and a tendency for the rider to bite their own tongue. This caused me to arrive, dust-splattered, grimacing and flecked with blood, looking like the survivor from a Biggles forced landing. It also had an outside flywheel carefully designed to chew lumps out of trousers and splatter hot oil as high as the kneecap. I bought it for thirty shillings, or one pound fifty from a railway porter named Alf. Now, Alf should have qualified for an Oscar as he confirmed what a bargain I had and how he would miss the fine machine which had been his reliable trusty companion. How gullible could I be?

This was a few months into the future on a beautiful May morning as we returned to work. The older men stretched where their muscles had stiffened after the short break. I was reluctant to disturb the peace of the valley, broken only by birdsong, including a persistent cuckoo who was offering his amorous services to any available female. Still, I started up the old diesel mixer. This was not quite as easy as it sounds, I would swing the starting handle. It resulted in a few puffs of evil blue-black smoke and a sigh from the engine. Nothing else, just a weary sigh. I would play with the lever for the cold start. Flick the brass decompression lever over and swing again. There would be so much fuel in the engine's bore that there would be a hydraulic lock and instant jolting failure. Eventually, it would start and settle down to a steady, rhythmic, smelly beat. If Ron were there, he would immediately take charge and frantically turn the handle with bulging cheeks and perspiration beading his brow. As his efforts reached bursting point, the drum of the mixer would turn, powered by manpower, not engine and old Uncle pushed his cap back and admired the effort, remarking that we could save money on fuel if Ron could keep it up for long enough to do a mix.

Occasionally, it would burst into life with the starting handle still in place. The heavy cast iron handle would whirl round and round, gaining momentum until centrifugal force hurled it into the air like a medieval weapon of war. Strangely, this normally only happened to Ron. Sometimes he would sink down exhausted and mop his brow because there was no sign of life. One youngster would take over, and it would start straight away. It would have started for Ron if he had checked that some joker had not sneaked the fuel tap off. The older tradesmen turned a blind eye to anything that was not too likely to cause danger to life or property, rightly putting things down to youthful high spirits.

Mostly, they were also cheerful and 'up for the crack' as we termed a laugh and joke. We, apprentices, were aware, though, that the same jovial workmates who tolerated our stupidity and played the same tricks on us, were also played on them by the previous generation. It was unbelievable to think, this was a generation where a mere fifteen or sixteen years ago they had been sliding a bayonet into a German's ribs or dropping by the dead of night into enemy territory. If we overstepped the mark, we could expect a 'slap', this being a euphemism for a full-blown punch. This ensured a little respect for them, and we knew where to draw the line.

Our older workmates tricked most of us.

'Quick! Go and ask the chippy (carpenter) for a long weight, don't hang about either, you idle little bugger,' would come the command. We would rush off knowing that sash windows operated with long tubular lead weights suspended from the cord.

'Let's have a long weight for Bert, please, he's in a right rush,' we would request.

'Hang on here, I'll be back' he growled. We would hang on. Hopping from one foot to another as the carpenter rummaged around. They would keep this charade going until we asked how much longer he would be with a triumphant grin he would say, 'You've had your long wait, now bog off you cheeky sod.' And we would trail back across the site with our workmates guffawing around us.

On one occasion we were working in a town, and they sent me over to an old-fashioned baker to buy fresh rolls and cakes. I enjoyed the errand. The smell of fresh bread was tantalising, and there was a mouth-watering selection of fresh cakes and pies. Behind the counter was a large cheerful blonde in her forties and a pretty shy girl a few years older than me. They sent me for all sorts of things I had never heard of, as well as the more common ones. One day it would be Apple tarts, the next Bakewell, Nelson squares would follow Bridies. The day that I asked if they had any Virgin tarts in the shop, I was totally unprepared for the ringing sensation in my ears.

I much preferred working in the country though, and fortunately, this was where our small firm mainly operated. Founded in the '30s by Fred as a one-man band, it had slowly expanded to include first his sons, then his son-in-law and finally a few outsiders. Fred was a dapper little man with the looks and demeanour of a weasel. His beady eyes would flicker around and finally settle on something to disapprove of. Maybe a pair of dirty boots when you arrived first thing in the morning. Then "pwash!" An explosion of air would release between his pursed lips, and his scrawny neck would shake from side to side. The weaselly whiskers of his grey moustache would project horizontally for a moment before he settled down to a steady whine that nobody listened to.

Fortunately, he left the day-to-day running of the firm to his eldest son Eric, who could not have been more of a contrast. He was a cheerful, tolerant man with unlimited patience. Eric had served as a commando during world war two but resisted all our attempts to persuade him to talk about his experiences. It was a period of his life that he wanted to draw a veil over. In many respects, he took after his uncle. Retired, we could persuade him to help when there was too much bricklaying to cope with. We all called him 'Uncle' although he was no relative of most of us.

The term suited him. A stocky avuncular figure, he would whistle cheerfully away, his weather-beaten cheeks looking in form, if not texture, for all the world like a cherub. His moustache was slightly longer than that of brother Fred's, but the grey was tinted ginger by the old pipe that remained clenched between his teeth when he was not whistling. At dinner break, he would produce a huge hunk of bread, and a horn handled penknife, then like a magician, from one of the sagging pockets in his ancient, leather patched jacket he would draw a piece of cheese wrapped in a twist of paper and an apple. He would cut bits off each and eat with all the relish of a man at a banquet before wiping his knife on his trousers, folding it away and lighting his pipe. This was a man at peace with himself and the world. Sometimes we were lucky, and Uncle's shoulders would shake with silent mirth. We waited expectantly, and he would chuckle and begin a story in his rich Hampshire accent that I will always regret never recording.

"Did I ever tell you about your Grandfather when Ee wuz in France?" he asked Nobby, the bricklayers hoddy or hod-carrier.

'Well, 'twere like this, they put me and a few others on a train for the last part of the journey up to the front, get us there quicker I suppose. I hadn't never been out of Hampshire before, let alone England, and I were pretty green. We gets off the train, which can't be done when you're in khaki wi'out a lot of roaring, shouting and a blowing of whistles. I looks over, and there is old Amos sittin' up on a horse an' cart lookin' like he wuz off to get the hay in down yonder field. He had bin sent down to pick up the officer's luggage see. The commotion wuz summat terrible an' all the while we could hear the thump of they big guns. Soon as I got a chance, I went over to your Grandad. I were that pleased to see a face that I knew. We gave each other a bit of news about the village an' that an' then I asks 'im if they guns always kep' a firin'. He pauses, pushed his helmet back an, says 'Arr what's think they'll keep on 'til they kills someone', never smiles, just flicks the reins and trundles on out'.

He chuckled again, 'Buggers never killed him, nor me though did' um?'

He described most of Uncle's war as being like a competitive football match; it was probably his way of coping with the true horror and slaughter. In civilian life, he was a keen shot, and many a rabbit fell foul of his gun. It was a talent he carried forward to his temporary career, and he exchanged the discomfort of the trenches for the certain death, in the event of capture, for a life as a sniper. He described a day when he leant against a tree a short distance from a stile. A German soldier hopped over the stile, briefly looked around, took off his helmet and lowered his trousers, 'I had'm' said uncle 'perfect shot.'

'Dead?' We asked. Uncle slowly shook his head, and again his shoulders shook, and he slapped his thighs in mirth.

'Said it were perfect, didn't I? Straight through the helmet what was hangin'' off the fence a foot away.' He leaps to his feet, shirttail a flappin', trousers 'round 'is ankles an' clears the fence like a two-year-old. Don't reckon he needed none of they syrup of figs though.'

When we persisted and asked him if he had seen any real horrors, he solemnly pressed the tobacco into his old pipe and after a few contemplative draws nodded. 'My brother there, see he played in the village band, still comes to that. When they calls him up, him not volunteering like me, they decides to put him in a band in a Scottish Regiment. I were on embarkation leave see when Fred comes marchin' 'ome. It were terrible 'im in a kilt with those little bandy legs of his, fair turned my stomach 'an the vicar's dog had a fit an all.'

There was little love lost between the two brothers, one of whom was as jocular as the other was bitter. It was ironic that Fred was deeply religious and a fervent chapel man. At the same time, Uncle was a beer-drinking, irreverent old reprobate who somehow made life better for everyone he came in contact with. The two old countrymen reminded me of Beatrix Potter figures, the irascible weasel vainly trying to irritate the kindly old badger.

You will never plough a field if you only turn it over in your mind - Irish Proverb

15

Wind in the Willows

In the late fifties and early sixties, there had been extraordinarily little new building in the old town, and it differed greatly from today. The town station closed long ago, and they have replaced the short length of line connecting it to the Junction station with dual carriageway, running beside a river populated with rusting supermarket trolleys from the shopping mall on the opposite bank. It was not always like this. Opposite the bus station, there was a narrow road leading down between the Co-Operative store and river to the old Town Mill. This road turned into a track that leads down to a market garden, which merged into watercress beds. On the opposite bank stood a cottage with a garden running parallel to the river. I was friendly with two brothers who lived here with their younger sister, mother, and father who ran the cress beds. At the top of the garden, by the cottage, was a landing stage with a punt and a boat moored up. This was a marvellous place to be. It was like living in the middle of the country, but actually being in the centre of town.

I spent a lot of time here, a Wind in the Willows life messing about in boats. One summer we had been swimming in the shallow river and were lying in a sun-filled meadow, studded with wildflowers, which is now a car park for a supermarket. We got to thinking 'What a pity the river was not as deep as it was in the winter when the floods raised the levels by a couple of foot and turned the lower part of the meadow into a pond.' Lying on our backs and

82

chewing a stalk of grass, we talked it over and gradually came up to build a dam. After all, if a beaver could do it, surely we could. As we talked, the plan took shape, and we met the following morning with saws, axes, and hammers.

There were a lot of old trees and shrubs around. We felled a few smaller trees and spent the first day sawing up poles and sharpening them to a point. Excitedly we met the following morning and, stripped to our swimming trunks, we hammered the poles into the river- bed, bracing them back down with diagonals. Each pole was about a yard apart and yard above water level, and they ran from bank to bank. The river was about two feet deep and moved at a lazy walking pace downstream.

We started filling in between the poles with branches woven like a giant basket and realized the pressure that the slow-moving water was applying. The dam was just above water level now, and the level had not seemed to rise, although it was pouring through the gaps like water from a giant watering can. Now for the final part of the plan. We had scrounged some old doors and sheets of corrugated iron, and we wedged these against the barricade and dug them into the bank each side of the river. Success! The water slowly rose toward the top of the bank about two feet above. On the opposite side of the makeshift dam, the water slowly dropped and finally became a pathetic six-inch deep stream slowing to a trickle. Eventually, of course, it would flow over the top and the level the other side of the dam would rise to normal.

We were jubilant; the plan was working. Soon we would have a private swimming pool to be proud of. It wasn't our river or our meadow that we were appropriating, but who would care? We were just about to find out. The level had dropped at the mill below, and two perplexed men were walking up the bed of the sadly diminished river in wellingtons, one of them with his cap pushed back on his head as he scratched it with the stub of a pencil. They came round the bend in the river and paused in amazement. The head-scratcher was the first to recover, and as he put two and two together, his face turned red, and he splashed up the stream towards us, waving his arms and cursing like an apoplectic hippo.

We stood our ground, well water then, on our side of the ramparts until he was about twenty feet away. Then the top of the dam bowed slowly out, poles lost their footing, and the ramshackle structure collapsed suddenly, sweeping us off our feet as several tons of water and assorted debris engulfed our would-be assailant. Fortunately, no one was hurt. That is my opinion. I'm sure he would have preferred it if the wreckage had keelhauled us before being drowned. His companion, who had seemed to be slower thinking proved us wrong. He swung himself up onto the bank with the aid of an overhanging branch and collapsed with helpless laughter as he watched us flounder about. We retreated upstream, and he hauled the hippo up on to the bank, sputtering and spitting out water weed. A strategic withdrawal seemed advisable. As we bolted across the now waterlogged meadow, we paused to watch as they made their escape downstream. As one struggled to pick bits of weed off his muddy jacket and the other slapped his thighs when our laughter permitted, we jauntily whistled the theme from the Dambusters.

Undaunted, but realising that building a dam was a little more technical than we had expected, we tried our hand at powerboating. At the bottom of the garden, there sat a small workshop housing a variety of tools, and we made our way down to it. Slowly the grand design fell into place, and using the materials we scrounged we built a boat. Imagine if you can a punt, oblong, not pointed at the end like a boat. The sides were scaffold planks. At the front, we cut a curve into each plank. From front to rear, we nailed a sheet of aluminium from the roof of an old caravan to the bottom of the planks.

The effect was that of a tiny landing craft. We lowered it into the water, and it sank until the top of the planks were only a few inches from the water level. We were over the moon, at least it floated, even if it looked more like a pram than a speedboat. We pulled it back out and raised the sides by nailing timber on top of the upright scaffold planks. Now for the bit, we were waiting for; we had an old engine from a Triumph motorbike. We mounted this on a wooden frame with a hinge at the front. By lifting the rear of the frame, we tilted the engine forward on the hinges. This raised the rear and tightened up a fan belt which drove a metal rod encased in a bit of old galvanised water pipe.

We used the blades from an old electric fan for a propeller. The ancient engine kicked into life and throbbed away happily. The noise from the open exhaust hiding the chattering from the make-do propeller shaft as the engine was tilted on its mounting and the fan belt tightened on the pulley. We were jubilant. There were a few minor details to sort out. The petrol tank from the motorbike was mounted on brackets above the engine, and the throttle was dispensed with. A piece of bailer twine served instead, straight out the top of the carburettor and tied to the tank mounting brackets. We held the maiden voyage straight away and sorted the details out later.

We lowered the ungainly craft gently into the river, and we piled in and prodded the obliging old engine into life, and the belt tightened, the engine promptly stalled. The fan we were using for the propeller was probably too big. By trial and error, we found that running the poor old engine at high revs and allowing the belt to slip let us get underway. Finally, we cast off, engine roaring and clouded in smoke from the engine and burning rubber until we were away. As momentum built up, we could tighten the belt by tilting the engine forward, and the speed increased. Move over, Bluebird! We were now moving at a fast trot, and the bows were clear of the water. Admittedly, all the weight was at the back, so it was not just down to speed. But this was what speed boats looked like! Bows in the air and stern down in the water. We roared down the river, scattering ducks and causing the donkey who lived in the meadow to kick up his heels in alarm.

The river ambled past the cress beds with meadows on the opposite bank for about a quarter of a mile until it reached the grounds of an old manor house used as offices by a large flour and animal feed organisation. The imposing old house stood in immaculate grounds with lawns stretching down to the river. There used to be a wooden bridge across the river, giving access to the gardens on the opposite bank. It was easy to imagine crinoline ladies, escorted by top-hatted gentlemen, tripping sedately across in its Victorian hey-day. We knew that it was possible to pass under the bridge in a rowing boat, by keeping to the middle and ducking our heads, so we approached the bridge at top speed. This would impress any onlookers. We aimed to shoot through these private grounds and pass under the road bridge at the far end into the next stretch of river, which again ran through cress beds. Too late we realised that the bows were out of the water higher than the bridge. Pandemonium broke out. The throttle could not be released because the baler twine was tied around the bracket, and the tilting engine mounting was wedged tight to prevent the belt from slipping. To steer we had brought an oar, this worked well in a rowing boat. We were about to learn that a flat-bottomed boat with no keel veers slightly to one side and carries on in a straight line like a demented crab when steered with an oar.

I can honestly say that the onlookers were impressed. We hit the bridge like a battleship ramming its opponent in an ultimate act of defiance. The wooden support cracked, and one side of the bridge sank into the water. The boat sank like a stone, steam and cracking noises coming from the abused engine and an oil slick spread downstream, for all the world like the doomed submarines we had seen in the films. The boat was referred to afterwards as the Titanic, and we never attempted to rebuild her.

I dread to think what the outcome would be now, no doubt insurance companies would be involved, charges of criminal damage brought, and even the owner of the old donkey in the neighbouring field would sue for the trauma to his prize animal. Then it was calmly agreed that we should pay for the materials and help the maintenance man rebuild the bridge. On a wage of under three pounds a week, it made a hole in our savings. However, we enjoyed our bridge-building, and it stood there for several years until the old house was slowly absorbed into the local college, the bridge dismantled, and the cress beds and meadows buried under a shopping mall. Sadly, tarmac and 'Kentucky-fried-Mac-Burgers' cover the meadows where buttercups and cowslips grew. And, ironically, a swimming pool now stands where we tried to build ours - an indoor, heated affair with lifeguards, safety restrictions, but no swallows or ancient donkey to watch the fun.

At last, I was sixteen and could ride a motorbike on the road, and the following summer peace returned to the river. John and I were now taking out twin sisters, and we would punt up the river and tie up under the overhanging branches of a weeping willow. The only sounds now were larks from the meadow behind, an occasional ripple and squawk from a protesting duck and the plop as a trout rose to suck down an insect from the swirling surface. The peace would be disturbed occasionally as a steam train chuffed up to the junction, and a trail of smoke would rise from above the willows.

Later, I bought a portable radio. This was not a transistor but a large battery-powered model with valves that took some time to warm up before the sounds of Craig Douglas asking the world why he had to be a teenager in love was added to the stillness of the summer evening. A young Cliff Richard had his turn too as he warbled about a "cryin' talkin' sleepin' walking, living doll." As this drowsy summer reached the end, smells of bonfires drifted over from the allotment and the chill of autumn caused us to shiver in the mist rising from the river. Slowly, the teenage romances also cooled, and we drifted apart, leaving the river to the mallards and the barn owl who haunted its banks like an extension of the swirling white wraiths of mist.

"Believe me, my young friend, there is nothing – absolutely nothing – half so much worth doing as simply messing about in boats." - Kenneth Grahame. Wind in the Willows

16

Making a Splash

We lived on a farm, with a cluster of cottages that lay between two villages. The common divides the two larger villages, and this is an extensive area of marshy grazing land known as Cow Common. In turn, wide tributaries of the River Test dissect the common. A footpath runs across and crosses the rippling chalk stream with wooden planked bridges. One of them, barely wide enough for two people to pass, with a handrail along one side, is perhaps twenty yards long and is predictably known as the long bridge. I have seen photographs taken at the turn of the century and very little seems to have altered on the common. The occasional horse and rider splash through. Excited dogs retrieve balls and sticks and then shake their shimmying bodies until a shower of water droplets to drench their owners with handfuls of diamonds. Cows amble across or lie in the shade on a hot summer day. Young lovers walk hand-in-hand, oblivious to the surrounding beauty, and occasionally, to the cow pats under their feet. This is no manicured village green, it is wide-open meadowland and remains relatively unspoiled, and long may it remain so.

If you visit early in the morning, you may well see a heron standing as if frozen into a graceful grey statue in the shallows. Or stalking like an anorexic ballet dancer through the marshy tufts, looking for a breakfast frog. If you disturb it, the heron takes to the air with slow strokes from powerful wings. It transforms into an ungainly hunchbacked figure by folding its neck, back, and legs up. The result resembles an overloaded 747 airliner laboriously gaining height until it rises above the treetops and cruises out of sight. Protected now, irate water keepers relentlessly shot heron's a few years ago to protect the fish stock. Although I know of a keeper who recently showed me the corpse of a heron remarking, 'He weren't very well protected against a twelve bore wuz he.'

Another creature that raised the keeper's blood pressure was the Otter. I am ashamed to say that I followed the otter hunt on more than one occasion as the terriers swarmed into and out of the river. They would tear around with the sort of grin that terriers get when encouraged to act outrageously. I never saw an otter caught, but it seemed an enjoyable way to work up a thirst (For everyone except the otter). For those not acquainted with otter hunting, I should explain that it involves dressing up. Usually, in green tweed with plus fours and socks held up with garters and coloured flashes similar to those worn by the boy scouts of yesteryear. They carry long staffs, probably to beat the reeds down or extricate the hunter from muddy patches. The indispensable item of equipment was a hip flask. They then pursued the elusive otters along the bank and river by a pack of milling, mud-spattered, excitable creatures of dubious parentage. The dogs were very similar. Watching people getting tipsy and fall in the river seemed a good way to spend the day when I was a schoolboy.

Things have 'improved' beyond recognition over the years. Now chemicals and pollution kill the wildlife, while the next generation expends as much energy trying to conserve life as their fathers did taking it. The average otter would probably prefer it if we tried to avoid killing him altogether, but he stood a better chance against terriers than he does against chemicals. To be fair, water quality has improved recently, as has the attitude toward otters, and I know of at least one local river where otters are seen.

I still visit the common quite often and find it busier than it used to be when I was young. Then there were fewer adults using it, and more children and teenagers. Parents are reluctant to allow their offspring to roam wherever they like on their own, and perhaps the children now prefer to spend their time on computers and play stations. We wandered where and when we liked and providing that we told our parents when we were returning, nobody worried. In fact, everyone knew where we were most of the time. Everybody knew everyone else. It was rare that the village policeman was not creaking around on his official, heavy-duty bicycle or one keeper was not around. I watched recently as two youths crossed the common. They were on mountain bikes and were obviously enjoying the exhilaration as they leapt in the air from a bank and splashed through the shallows. A small group of elderly walkers shook their grey heads, and one of them gesticulated angrily. I could imagine the conversation, 'Youth of today,' 'Should never be allowed!' 'banned,' 'danger,' etc. Where did these people come from? Unless they had terrible memories, they could not have been locals because these lads were only a modern version of us.

To the north of the common, the ground rises onto downland and eventually flattens out onto the site of a WW2 airfield. The road winds through the village, past the farm and church at the lower end and by the thatched cottages and pub. Running parallel with the river and rising, as it skirts the edge of the common, the route is idyllic. As it leaves the village, it still runs parallel with the river but is now level with the tops of the horse chestnut trees below. There used to be a wooden seat on a flat part of the grassy verge where you could sit and watch the sun glint off the ripples as the swans glided by. The grassy bank dips down so sharply to the river it is not possible to climb down without using hands to scrabble at the tufts of grass. It was possible, for the brave or foolhardy, to launch oneself over the edge on a bicycle and plunge to the bottom. It was pointless to use brakes, the back wheel would just lock solid and skid, and the front would throw you over the handlebars. The art was to apply full brakes as you reached the narrow strip of grassy bank beside the river and wrench the handlebars round to turn the bike into a sideways skid. You would end standing on the pedals and accelerating off. Get it wrong, and you were in the river. Brake too late and you went in headfirst. Break too early, and the bike stayed on the bank but catapulted you into the water. If you were just unlucky, you got it nearly right and went in sideways. When there was an audience ready to hurl derisory comments, and you just knew it had gone wrong, it was customary to lift hands and feet in the air and let out a whoop like an Indian Brave. At this point, you would make a spectacular splash and emerge soaking wet and dripping with weed. This made it possible to pretend that you had done it on purpose. This didn't fool anyone. Particularly when in the middle of winter or when you were wiping off a mixture of blood and mud. But it enabled you to save face.

One-by-one we graduated from bicycles to motorbikes, mainly old oily wrecks that were well past their prime, and inevitably it was only a matter of time before someone went hurtling down the bank on a motorbike. Most of the old four-stroke motorcycles had a lever on the handlebars that lifted the valves and made it easier to kick start the engine. We learned that if we used this, it slowed the descent without locking up the back wheel. A stamp on the back brake at the bottom of the hill, turn the handlebars, and the rear end would skid round. Open the throttle and away in a shower of mud and pebbles and along the bank until the gradient was shallow enough to blast up it back up onto the road.

A group of us had gathered one evening when we were joined by a lad, known for some reason as, Bilge. Although he was the same age as us, we did not know him well because he went to boarding school. We had bought our own bikes with money earned from a variety of jobs. Bilge had his given to him as a sixteenth birthday present. It was a brand new BSA Bantam, immaculate in its shiny grey paint. He tossed his head disdainfully as he viewed our motley collection of smoking wrecks and lit up a filter-tipped cigarette with a silver lighter. He was annoying us. Barry was trying to push the loose ends of tobacco back into a deformed, skinny roll-up with the end of a swan vesta. He threw down the gauntlet, literally and metaphorically. 'Let's see you ride down the bank then.' A chorus of jeers, hoots and chicken impressions backed him until Bilge finally agreed. We formed a group around him at the top, and Barry held his rear wheel to stop him from leaving before he was ready. White-faced and white-knuckled, Bilge paused at the top until we said, 'Go,' and launched him into space. Straight as an arrow, he sped, and we clung to each other in gales of helpless laughter. Just before the bottom Bilge, let go of the handlebars and let out a mighty "GERONIMO." A split second later, he disappeared in a cloud of steam. We scrambled down the bank and stood clapping and cheering as he emerged like Neptune from the depths with his fists held in a prizefighter's triumphant clasp above his head. We helped him to fish his bike out of the shallow water and clapped him on the back. Bilge had joined the club.

'Could have done it easily, of course,' he said later.

'Just thought you chaps deserved a laugh!' Barry knew differently. As a precaution, he had undone the brass nut on the rear brake rod when he was 'assisting' by holding the back wheel, so his poor victim had no rear brake. Still, we had to give credit where it was due, and Bilge had achieved the most spectacular failure to date. Bilge gained so much confidence that it was a miracle that he survived... his exploits became legendary. One day he rammed a milk float in the side and sailed through the open sides. He glided over the top of the stacked milk crates and earned himself a few days in the hospital. This may be what prompted his choice of career because he came back misty-eyed over nurses. We lost touch after he went to university. He moved out of the area and eventually became a doctor.

My memory stirred again. There was something uncannily familiar about the silver-haired man about the same age as Bilge would be now, shaking his fist at the departing youths on their mountain bikes. Impossible, surely, but he looked just like Bilge's old grandfather!

17

The Irish Rover

As we worked, Uncle explained what we were doing, 'Taint no use using cement, boy this was built with lime, same as Romans did, this 'ere lime lets it breath see, lets it move around a bit an' all, that's why we use six shovels of sand and one of lime, no durn'd cement.' He was right, of course, and now it is possible to pay a lot of money to go on conservation courses to learn what his elders had taught him. On these courses you will not get the folklore and insight into the past that we were paid to absorb, nor will you get the fund of stories that came from a boyhood spent in an isolated Hampshire village in the 1880s. I was fascinated. He was a marvellous storyteller, and after the mixer stopped, there was virtual silence apart from birds, the occasional low hum of a distant tractor and the scrape and chink of the trowels.

Uncle would tell us that in his youth, they would have pushed the tools and a few materials on a two-wheeled cart from the village in the valley where he still lived. If it were more than an hour's walk, they would often sleep in the barn during the week, cooking food over an open fire and washing in the stream. Horse and cart would deliver materials. He was possibly one of the last generations in this part of the world to live in a world where the horse was king, and he was a link with the past for me.

He also taught me that my generation had not invented sex. By all accounts, Victorian attitudes had not penetrated true rural areas. His eyes would twinkle away as he recalled escapades with village girls who were now respectable grandmothers who frowned on our lifestyles, 'She weren't no better than what she ought to be, why I mind the time....' The tale would get worse, and we would listen, laughing out loud while the exploits of Churchwardens, retired Head Mistresses, Dairymaids and staid respectable Farmers became revealed. History became live when Uncle was speaking, and I realized that although there were poverty and hardship, there was also satisfaction and friendship. He made us realise that, yes, we were lucky, but that his generation and his father's generation had nothing to compare their lives with, so according to Uncle, they were happy. They made their own amusements. Many were talented musicians. They enjoyed a drink when they could get one, and a puff of tobacco chased the girls and caught a few. It sounded familiar enough to me. In this way, I gained a link with the past and realised that the world three hundred years before was probably little different from the world of Uncle. In another two or three hundred years when they come to repair what we built that day, it will be a different story. They will inhabit a different world. Hopefully, they will preserve the tradition of wine, women, and song; though they can skip the tobacco by all means.

The two brothers spoke in the dialect that their fathers and forefathers had used in the isolated community for generations. As I said, I will always regret the fact that I never taped the conversations; their sons had already lost the true vocabulary that would enable us to know how our rural ancestors sounded. For instance, the small snack normally eaten at tea break was referred to as 'Nammit', a confused person was 'Puggled', woodlice were 'Pollywogs', although this meant tadpole in many areas. Dialect words were in common use; 'How bist?' was a way of asking how you were if something didn't work; they would say that it didn't 'Acle'. Acle could be substituted for work, fit, operate or sound right and can occasionally be heard now when one man is establishing his origins. If met with a blank stare, you know that you are not dealing with a local. The customary greeting would be, 'Alright you?'

'Yeah, what's on you?' would come the response. Conversations like,

'What'think they'm a-goin' t' plant they taters afore Easter'

'Casn't credit it, 'taint rhyme nor reason to it, they be gwan to be shrammed with frost ennum?' were held all day and would be easily understood by us and interpreted as 'There is no sense in planting your potatoes too early, the frost might catch them.' Phrases such as, 'They are going to town, aren't they?' would be rendered as, 'They'm gwoin' t' town bennam?'

We thought nothing of this until we were joined by an Irishman named Harry. He was an educated man with a soft Southern accent. Nobody enquired why such a man was working for a building company nor where he learned to play so many musical instruments with such skill, a man's past was his affair. There was one problem, the language barrier. I had no difficulty. As a child, I had lived all over the British Isles and could understand most people. Everyone but the two brothers could understand the soft lilting tones of Harry, but the Hampshire dialect was a closed-door to him. Fred was quick to weigh up the situation. He listened for maybe ten seconds and then cocked his head on one side like a sparrow, 'Yerr, you'm Oirish ain't you?'

We translated, and Harry confirmed softly, 'I am.'

Fred nodded with satisfaction, 'Thought thee wur thee talks queer don't 'ee'.

Harry persevered with the language and after a few months could understand most of the conversation, though he was prone to shaking his head in amazement and muttering 'They think I talk strangely.'

What finally fazed Harry was when the brothers were referring to a village called Knights Enham. Fred turned to Uncle and said, 'How 'bout t' others, they'm goin' to Enham b'ennum?'

Meaning. 'Are the others going to Knights Enham?' Harry's eyes glazed over, then he flung his cap on the floor and jumped up and down on it.

'I'll never learn this heathen language,' he yelled.

'The ennums and bennums have a life of their own to be sure.'

He spoke in Gaelic to the two brothers for a week, but it was totally wasted. It made no more sense than his normal speech did to them.

Just after this, we were sent to work at an enormous house owned by a well known aristocratic family in a village just over the border in Berkshire. The drive to work was a pleasure in many ways. Many builders were transported in what looked like a tin hut. It was like a small Nissan hut roped onto the back of a lorry, and their day started bouncing up and down on a planked seat. We rode in a Bedford mini-bus that seated twelve in comfort. In those days nearly everyone smoked and sometimes it was hard to see through the swirling clouds of pipe and cigarette smoke, but if it were warm enough, we would have a window open and watch the changing countryside as it rolled past. A few miles out of the village the Bedford would change down a gear, and we would climb a long drag to the summit. There, on top, was a large old house standing on a plateau. There was a fantastic view as we dropped down the other side, and it was surprising how the weather would often change at this point. We would climb up in brilliant sunshine and drop down in mist, or vice versa. The large house had been an inn for several years and would have provided welcome relief for travellers by foot or horse. We used to speculate about highwaymen and tales of past adventures. "Come on, Uncle, you must know a story," we pressed our historian.

"Argh," he confirmed. "Reckon I do an' all."

Sure of his audience, he told the tale of two women who lived in the small hamlet that lay just out of sight to the side of the inn. All their lives these two had been bitter enemies. Some forgotten girlhood slight had festered and grown into hatred. Now in their sixties on a late November evening, when the top of the hill was clouded in a blanket of fog, the enmity between the two widows reached a breaking point. They grimly stepped from the warm inn where they had been drinking at opposite ends of the room, into the gloomy night. The Landlord was heard to say that in his heart, he knew that only one would come back. A fiendish shriek and a cackle of laughter tore the night sky. The mini-bus was as silent as the inn had been on that winter night. 'How did she kill her?' I finally inquired. 'Kill her, what do you mean Kill her?' said Uncle.

'They settled it ladylike, upped with their skirts and squatted on the brow of the hill. One who's piddle ran furthest got to choose which night she was drinking on Friday or Saturday'.

I threw my lunch bag at Uncle, but I did him wrong as it proved to be a true story.

We drove another ten miles or so, passed through the small market town with its cottage hospital and a queue of nurses waiting at the bus stop. Crisp uniforms and black stockings provoking the normal response from the lads and a scurrilous tale from Uncle about life and love in a French field hospital. Out into open country again and wind through lanes led us to a gatehouse and private road. Iron railings enclosed magnificent cedars, and an air of privileged nobility reigned. The mansion was imposing, even more so was the ruined castle. No longer inhabited but owned by the present family since the civil war.

We were greeted by the Lord himself, who was a gentleman of the old school, and being an ex-soldier knew the value of keeping the troops well fed. Accordingly, he led us round to the tradesman's entrance and into the kitchen. 'Cook I'm sure you will find these chaps something at lunchtimes, maybe a bowl of soup even?' He lifted a languorous hand and as a contrast marched off, leaving us in the hands of Cook. Rarely have I seen anyone look so unimpressed as that cook. If a rat had popped out of the larder, it would have received a rapturous reception compared to us. We felt as welcome as a turd in a swimming pool, as Harry elegantly put it later. In looks, Harry resembled a garden gnome and had the build of a badly stuffed teddy bear. We all liked him, and he could make us smile, but Mr Matinee idol he was not. We were unprepared for what happened next.

An angelic smile lit up his face, and a million megawatts of Irish charm knocked the legs from under the scowling cook, within minutes she was giggling like a schoolgirl and Harry was washing up dishes and regaling her with tales of Ireland in between singing snatches of romantic songs. He shushed us out of the kitchen, sympathising all the while about the unappreciated hardworking staff, and gave us a wink. The food was superb; we had an unlimited supply of tea and coffee for the six months that we worked there. When the weather turned colder, we enjoyed roast pheasant, the occasional glass of fine wine and the odd culinary treat that cook pronounced 'Too good for them upstairs'. The Lord had a superb job done, the cook looked years younger, and Harry established himself as a legend. Even Uncle was deeply impressed.

We worked in a lot of manors and mansions belonging to the 'old money' families. In one of them, there was a series of long, highly polished oak floored corridors. Everyone was neurotic about damage to these and every night when the dust sheets were removed we ran up and down them with buffers on long poles, not content with this the domestic staff would re-polish in the morning before we sheeted up again. Those floors gleamed, they glowed with the patina that two hundred years of hard work can give, they were also like ice rinks. During the summer, the family went to the south of France for a few months' holiday, and the house was running on a skeleton staff. Harry had worked his customary magic on the housekeeper, and she found him a few 'cast-offs' belonging to the wealthy owner. In fact, we were getting used to him coming to work in immaculate Turner and Asbull shirts. He soon stopped coming on the van each evening and would greet us each morning standing in the carved doorway, smoking a Havana cigar, and looking as if it was his natural surroundings. It surprised us when we were stopped in the door one morning, though.

'Something different today lads, sure the work can wait awhile. It's race day, and I've opened a book. Honest Harry. That's your man, now let's see the colour of your money.'

I don't suppose we should have been surprised when Harry opened up the cardboard box. Inside were three tortoises, each with a blob of coloured paint on their shell.

'Now lads show these fine animals the course. They're champing at the bit, 'said Harry, placing the tortoises at the end of the corridor. We went along with the joke and gave Harry our shillings, betting on the blue, green or red as the fancy took us and prepared to walk away and come back in a couple of hours to find the winner. "They are off!" called Harry, picking up a three-foot broom and sweeping the unsuspecting animals down the shiny corridor. They shot away down the long polished oak floor and accelerated past an astonished Labrador who skidded with legs scrabbling wildly after his unusual quarry. We thought afterwards that it might have been cruel, but such was the power of our bookie that he stood with shining eyes and said, 'Look lads, the little creatures enjoyed it. All of their lives plodding along and getting nowhere. Sure, this is the stuff of their dreams, something to tell their grandchildren about, the only high-speed tortoise. Imagine the thrill of a bobsleigh run for one of these poor plodding creatures. Broaden your minds; live the dream.'

We went away laughing. Strangely, though I can't remember Harry paying any money out.

* * *

By now I was seventeen, I had a bit of money saved and also worked on what we called 'Privates'. These were cash jobs not connected to the company and done in the evenings and weekends. It was a privilege to be invited to do one of these by your workmates, a rite of passage that recognised that you were fast enough to earn your share of the money, not just get a wage, regardless. My old motorbike was a museum piece, and now I wanted another. I was enthralled by a maroon Triumph five hundred twin and gave in. The ride to work was now a pleasure, and sometimes I would make my own way to the job for the sheer joy of sweeping around the winding roads, smelling the wildflowers and feeling the air on my face. Particularly in the late summer when I could feel the air temperature change as I swooped up and down hills breathing in the familiar smells of harvest. Sometimes a fat beetle that we called harvest bugs would come the other way, and it was surprisingly painful... Especially if it hit you in the face, I arrived a couple of times with a fat lip.

I now need to explain, the amount of freedom in the late nineteen fifties would be unbelievable to the motorcyclist of today. The rules were simple. Buy a license, buy a bike, insure it, tax it, ride it. Yes, that was it. It was possible to ride any sort or size of bike on even a provisional licence. There were no speed limits on the roads outside built-up areas. Unbelievably, there was no M O T-tests, and no law compelling you to wear a crash helmet, yet an astonishing number of us survived.

One of my favourite rides to work took me close to the American Airbase at Greenham Common. We were working on a large Regency house, standing in its own grounds close to the small river to the south of the common. It had been bought by a fairly young business tycoon and his gorgeous wife. They had two children, both under school age, and had wisely rented a house nearby while we ripped their new acquisition apart. At one time all the drainage was out of action as we altered pipe runs and re-routed sewers. Life was a little more basic in the building industry in those days, not for us the luxury of Portaloos emptied weekly on contract. We had the time-honoured 'bucket and chuck it'.

We had a huge galvanised bucket in a small wooden shed complete with a wooden seat with a suitably sized hole. A newspaper would be torn into squares and impaled on a rusty nail inside the door and, hey presto, toilet facilities. The snag was of course that someone had to dig a hole and empty the bucket down it then fill the hole back in. All totally bio-degradable and a centuries-old solution. I was used to this; we still used this method at the old farmhouse where I lived. That was fortunate because the rule was the youngest emptied the bucket. Fair enough, for a fair proportion of the winter, I carefully lifted the turf in the paddock, dug a hole and emptied the bucket, filled the hole and replaced the turf. It was a neat job if I say so myself. It was impossible to see where I had been. Winter turned into spring, normal toilet facilities were restored, and the paddock was a sea of golden daffodils and pale nodding narcissi. Even the gardener agreed that it was a fine show. The job finished in early summer and the gardener put in a magnificent effort. The new owners arrived with their children, and everything was pristine.

The paddock had been mown the day before, and appreciative and satisfied eyes swept the magnificent view. We did not notice before, but now the grass was cut there were darker patches of more luxuriant grass where the buckets had been emptied and the turf replaced. Children miss nothing. A small voice piped up, 'Mummy, what are those marks in the grass.'

'Oh, darling,' the innocent mother exclaimed.

'How lovely they are fairy circles.' Uncle choked and clapping me on the back chortling. 'Argh, and here's your fairy.'

Mother looked baffled, and the small son regarded me solemnly, indelibly fixing in his mind the picture of a red-faced fairy dressed in a black leather jacket, jeans, and leather boots. It may have confused him, possibly not considering the later connotation of fairy.

18

The Ferret and Firkin

The snow crunched under the tyres of my motorbike as I cautiously turned off the main road and gently twisted the throttle open to cross the bridge over the steel grey river sparkling below. I pulled up outside the cottage of my friend, swung a leg over the saddle and heaved the bike onto its stand. Pulling the leather gauntlets off, I crouched down for a moment and warmed my hands on the engine. My friend's father popped his head over the hedge 'Thought it was you, Ian, he said.

'Nippers inside getting his breakfast. Go on in 'spect there's some bacon for you if you're quick'.

'Thanks. How about you?' He smiled.

'I was up early this morning, had mine before first light. That last shower of snow was too much for the old elm tree, brought a branch down, straight across our khazi, knocked it down to pan height!'

I looked across at the little wooden shed that housed the toilet bucket. It was leaning drunkenly, and two lengths of timber propped the sides up. There was an old door resting on top with two sandbags holding it down. 'That'll do until I get some proper wood and a sheet of corrugated tomorrow,' he said. I smiled, and he grinned back. Never one to be flustered, he made the best of it.

'Every cloud has a silver lining, they say. Got a bit more wood for the fire now, at any rate—one thing about logs. You get three good warmings out of them. One when you chop it down, one when you saw it up, and another when you burn it. Not that I had to chop this beggar down, nature did that for me.'

I nodded, 'Could do with a bit of heat I reckon, it's colder than it's been all winter.'

He brushed the snow off his woollen gloves. 'Got to expect it... February innit? Know what they say, 'when the days get longer, the cold gets stronger.'

'Where are you two off to then?'

'We were going to the motorbike scramble over at Owlesbury' I replied. 'But the roads are worse than I thought though, and I reckon we'll give it a miss, they'll probably cancel it, anyway.'

'You'll be daft if you go. Look at that sky, yellow over the trees and colour of lead above. Mark my words, Mother'll be plucking the goose again before noon. Still, she'll be chucking enough feathers down to put a few inches on the roof of our old thunderbox. That'll help keep the draughts out.'

As usual, he was right. By midday, large flakes swirled gently down, for all the world like the feathers he had so accurately forecast. I slid the mile back home, trailing my feet and prodding to keep the bike upright. Looking back, it is surprising how often the old weather sayings were right.

'Red sky at night shepherds delight; Red sky in the morning shepherds warning.'

'Rain before seven, fine before eleven.' To a generation who earned their living out of doors in all weathers, there were many signs.

'Swallows flying high, staying dry,'

'Frog hopping, rain dropping.' Others were strictly local and perfectly accurate.

'If you can hear the train before it gets to Bunny Bridge, you're in for a wet back.' This was a steam train, and it seemed to be true that sound carried better just before the rain. The saying was right more often than not, anyway.

We decided that the best place to be in foul weather was the public bar of the local. The pub has changed its name now, like many others. Then it was a sensibly named pub for drinkers. It was possible to get a plate of bread and cheese with homemade pickle or an onion at lunchtime, but in the evening the only food available was a packet of crisps with the addition of a pickled egg dropped in. There was no jukebox, just an ancient piano that an unlikely assortment of musicians played. The dartboard was in constant use with the ring of holes on the wood panelling behind the well-worn board, proving that strong ale was not a guarantee of better performance. They scattered a motley collection of tables throughout the bar, and nearly every one was occupied with domino or crib players. Each evening, players hunched over tabletops and cleared a space between their glasses and ashtrays. They would then settle down to the strange scoring, which remained unintelligible to the uninitiated.

On another were a polished shove halfpenny board and an old beer mug containing halfpennies, some of which dated from Victorian days, worn as smooth as a baby's bum as the locals said. A few old armchairs were pulled up around the fireplace. We youngsters knew better than to take one of them. Some old regulars reserved these, and the old chaps appeared most evenings, walking, or shuffling, to the bar expecting the landlord to have the 'usual' ready for him. These privileged patrons each had their own glass or tankard hung in a row above the bar, and they were sacrosanct. There was even a battered old pewter tankard that had been hanging there since the First World War. The owner had never returned from France, but as the landlord held, 'he said he'd be back, and no one knows for sure.'

Some really old boys still dressed up to come down the pub and had waistcoats with watch chains festooned across the front and shiny boots. They viewed us with scorn in our jeans and denims. I remember one evening parking my bike outside and walking up to the bar. There was a group of ancients gathered there, and I nodded to them as I put my half-crown down and ordered up a pint of Simmonds Nut Brown ale. One of them turned to me and slowly looked me up and down, then he turned sad eyes to his companions, slowly raised his glass of best bitter and blew the froth off the top all over me. 'We sprays leather-jackets round 'ere,' he proclaimed, wiping the rest of the froth off his walrus moustache. This produced gales of mirth from the whole pub who appreciated the pun on the larvae of the caddis fly. I am sure that Marlon Brando would have come up with a suitable reply if his leather jacket was sprayed with froth, but I just joined in the joke against me and laughed with the rest.

There was a lot of 'Micky-taking' then. Most of it was harmless fun, not politically correct, and most of it likely to offend now. By the end of the evening, the pub was often rocking with laughter and singing, but hardly ever any unpleasantness. There were a few characters, but we were used to their ways. Those unfamiliar with the interactions were taken aback, especially when old Shep used to spit his false teeth in his pint glass before venturing outside to the toilet. This ensured nobody had a sly drink out of his glass. Unnervingly he did this in a flamboyant way, holding his glass at arm's length and spitting at a distance. He had a weak bladder, so he had plenty of practice.

Tommy used to approach a victim who had just bought a pint, roll his eyes and let his jaw hang open and fix him with a stare. 'Bet you a shilling I could drink that without spilling a drop or touching it with my hands.' The stranger would consider this for a moment and either not want to get in an argument with the village idiot, or he was confident of winning. 'Bet you can't.' As soon as they made the bet, Tommy would snatch the glass in both hands down the pint in one, wipe his mouth on the back of his hand, and hand over a shilling. 'You win,' he would say, leaving the victim to buy another pint for over twice the price.

There were no lager louts. But, come to think of it, there was no lager! You could drink bitter, light and bitter, mothers-in-law (that is stout and bitter for the uninitiated), and mild beer from the keg or bottled brown, pale light or stout. It was to be several years before I heard of lager and we laughed at the thought of it selling. Especially when rumoured that some drinkers in the lounge bar drank out of half pint glasses, but that was a different world. One thing was the same in each bar. The ceilings were always the same shade of brownish yellow, stained with nicotine from countless cigarettes and pipes and tinted by the smoke from the logs crackling away in the fireplace. They were unhealthy places, pubs; I bet there was hardly a man over ninety in ours.

There were many pubs like this; then, there were also other types. Some of them were 'Olde Worlde' with horse brasses on the wall that had never seen a horse and sporting prints with the ink barely dry on them. The car park outside would have shiny Rovers or sporty MG's outside. Tweed-clad men, some of whom brought their wives with them, would inhabit the bar. We rarely invaded their territory, and apart from the younger ones who played for the cricket team, they never invaded ours.

By the sixties, things changed, though. The old boys were fighting a losing battle, bars were brightening up, and we started taking girls into pubs. There were advertisements on the bar for Babycham and Cherry B. Some pubs even started selling food, and the smell of scampi and chips competed with tobacco smoke. This didn't meet with approval from many who regarded the pub as a refuge from domesticity. It was inhibiting too. Men did not swear in the company of women, and the language in the bar was the language of the barrack-room or building site.

In most cases, the migration of 'the new wave' into the lounge bar, with its newly fitted carpet and jukebox, resolved it. Some say this was the beginning of the end for the traditional pub. Yet, a few resisted to the bitter end.

One evening about ten years ago, I was drinking in a country pub in a small village close to Winchester. The clientele was much as it was when I was a youth, but with the addition of some stable girls, accepted as 'one of the boys' because of their ability to down pints and out-swear the men. The atmosphere was raucous and smoky, and the floorboards were bare with the patina of spilt pints and muddy boots. It was a breath of fresh air. The door opened, and a man and woman, both strangers, stepped in, shaking the raindrops from their shoulders. The man approached the bar and requested, "Do you serve snacks?" Without a trace of irony, the landlord nodded "Of course, what would you prefer? Salt and vinegar or plain?"

I sat watching and smiling to myself as I listened in on a group of men seated around a table. I could tell this was an interesting one to sit and watch as I supped on my pint. One of them was wearing a scruffy old jacket of indiscriminate colour, an organic type of jacket, the colour of something growing on a stone in a dank wood. He reached into his pocket and produced a young ferret which he let slip through his hands a few times before placing it on the tabletop. The ferret sinuously wound itself around the glasses a few times before returning to his owner. 'Any of you want to buy a ferret?' asked the proud owner. The animal and man looked around. 'You can see how tame he is. Do you a treat for rabbits or quiet enough for a pet.' They all nodded, and one stroked the ferret tentatively. A florid faced man dipped his finger in his pint and thrust it out. The ferret licked it with every sign of enjoyment. Rocking with laughter, the red-faced gent dipped his finger in the glass again and held it out to the animal. With all the speed of a striking cobra, the ferret sank his teeth into the extended finger. Glasses went flying as the victim leapt to his feet with a bleeding finger clamped under his armpit. 'Bloody animal! Dangerous that's what that is, shouldn't be allowed to bring wild animals into a pub!' The owner calmly slipped the ferret back into the sagging jacket pocket and retorted 'Wasn't wild 'till you got the poor little sod pissed, was he?'

19

Firm's Outing

Perhaps you remember that I mentioned Dick, the singer of strange Canadian melodies? He worked with us and smiled at the antics of the youngsters, after all, he suffered the bombastic Ron too. Dick was a quiet, gentle man, but sometimes when we were doing a boring job, he would start talking, and we would hear more tales of life in rural Hampshire. He lived in the same village as Uncle, in a cottage that I eventually bought off him. It lay in a valley with a steep hill into the village. A few houses strung along the main road and a steep climb back out. The hillsides, partly covered with ancient woodlands, and partly with grassy downland, were too steep to cultivate. Either by the horses of the pre-war era, or the chugging Fordson Major and little grey Ferguson tractors that the local farmers favoured. At the valley bottom, the cottages spread left and right, up and down the small bourne that meandered along through a series of picturesque villages that had changed little since Uncle was a boy. Cows grazed the valley bottom, mainly the familiar black and white Friesians, medium-sized cattle with a justified reputation for a high milk yield, and sheep grazed the steep slopes and had for centuries. Dick's father had been a shepherd, living on the outskirts of the village for most of the time and in a shepherd's hut at lambing time. Shepherds huts were substantial wooden huts mounted on cast iron wheels, rather like a primitive caravan. They had a basic wooden bed and a potbellied, cast- iron stove inside for heating and cooking, and the shepherd shared the arrangement with his dog.

Shortly after lambing, one job for the shepherd is to castrate the male lambs. This is a humane affair now, but in the days when Dick's father was a shepherd, it was the job of the shepherd, either with his trusty knife or, so we were told, by the shepherd's teeth. Much in the same way that an umbilical cord is bitten through, the shepherd would castrate the unfortunate animal. He would throw the results to the impatient collie who stood yelping with anticipation or spit them into a frying pan that sizzled away on the corner stove. Although hardened to the realities of rural life, this seemed barbaric even to us.

Dick had inherited some of his father's talents. Sometimes, a neighbour asked him to castrate a Tomcat - Dick had perfected a technique. He would pick Tom gently up, and before the reality of the situation had struck, he was slid headfirst into a Wellington boot and emasculated with a swift stroke of a safety razor. Amazingly, they seemed to suffer more indignity than distress. Dick's dexterity was legendary, and one day, when asked to perform this delicate operation by a neighbour, and the customary fee of a packet of Woodbine cigarettes negotiated, Dick called round with the tools of his trade the following evening. Always a man of his word, he presented himself at his neighbour's house and there sunning himself on the front lawn was a fine specimen of a cat. Dick was actually very fond of cats and tickled its ears before gently sliding the unsuspecting animal into the Wellington boot and performing the deed. He emptied Tom out of the boot who quick as disappeared over the horizon like a bullet. Dick knocked on the door. There was no reply, so he strolled off home for tea with all the satisfaction of a job well done. Later that evening, there was a knock at the door. There on the doorstep stood his neighbour. 'Sorry, I wasn't in earlier. I've brought the cat'. Dick viewed the small white cat held out to him. Even the shock of the operation would not have transformed the huge tabby he had performed on earlier, into the patient he was now being offered. The look of shock and horror on Dick's face equalled that of the bemused tabby that was in the wrong place, at the wrong time.

Eric was a good boss with views, fairly advanced for the day. One of these was the concept of a work's outing. He decided that we needed our horizons expanding and arranged a trip up to London just before Christmas one year. We were 'dead chuffed'. I had never been to London, nor had Nobby or Joe, my contemporaries, and we eagerly awaited the day. Eric issued strict instructions. 'Dress smart, van leaves at seven sharp, bring a bit of money but you won't need much. The treat is on the firm.' When we turned up, Nobby was in drape jacket and drainpipe trousers, and Joe and I donned clean jeans and leather jackets, trying to look like Marlon Brando in 'The Wild Bunch'. Our workmates had excelled themselves.

Eric dressed in a blazer and grey flannels, with his hair just beginning to grey 'looked the part' with his regimental tie and embroidered blazer badge telling the world that here was an ex-serviceman and proud of it. His younger brother, the affable and slightly more rotund Larry, wore a similar outfit. His R.A.F. tie., and his Brylcreem hair proclaimed his branch of the service. Dick wore a pullover and open-neck shirt but looked scrubbed and dapper. And dressed in a shiny 'de-mob' suit (as they called the free issue given to returning servicemen after the war), Ron for once in his life was restrained. There was no way that Uncle was going to miss this treat, and he stood puffing on his pipe. His black boots were shining, his gold watch chain glistened across his ample middle, and he stood proudly in a navy-blue suit neatly pressed, even if it did smell of mothballs. His eyes twinkled merrily, and his snowy white eyebrows stood out against his weathered brown brow. I had never seen him without his antique cap, but today he wore a bowler hat borrowed from the farmer who judged the cattle show. He looked like a man from another century, which of course he was.

I had seen Harry dressed-up before, and he usually wore an extraordinary tweed suit of a totally shapeless design. Fashioned of various shades of moss green tweed with short grey hairs, like a redundant toothbrush sticking out in all directions, it reflected his country-gent look. But not today. Today dressed for 'town' he sported a Victorian velvet smoking jacket, pristine white cricket trousers and patent leather dancing shoes - on anyone else it would have looked ridiculous. We gaped in amazement at our bohemian leprechaun, but with total aplomb, he settled down in the van, drew out a mouth organ and played. After a few of the Simmonds nut brown ales from the crates provided by Eric, he confessed that he had spent the previous night at a 'lady friends' house and had left it too late to go back to his lodgings and change. This latest love of his was 'in service' at a large house, the owners were away, and Harry had 'borrowed' his outfit picking clothes that the elderly gentleman was unlikely to miss.

The sixty-mile journey passed quickly enough, singing and smoking, entertained by Uncle's tales and the expert playing of Harry. We paced our drinking as we wanted to be more or less sober when we reached London and piling into a Transport Café at Staines for breakfast helped. The lorry drivers showed no surprise when twelve ill-assorted inebriated, merrymakers ranging in age from seventy-plus to seventeen invaded their domain playing the mouth organ, spoons and comb and paper to give a lively rendition of 'Danny Boy' at breakfast time. Still, the café owner's wife restored order and cheerfully threatened us with a frying pan.

So, well-fed and watered, we drew into London, parked up on a side street in Hounslow. There were no meters then, of course, and we caught the tube into 'town'. I don't know what London made of us, but we loved London. Eric knew his way around, and we saw most of the familiar landmarks and many unfamiliar pubs. Swaying gently, we arrived at Harrods for lunch, another treat from Eric. It was just before Christmas and all the decorations adorned the shops, and exotic treats were all around. We lads had never been in a shop larger than the local Co-op and this strange treasure store fascinated us. Our elders smiled superior smiles, but they were equally enthralled. Then we found the toy department, Harry swooped on a toy whistle and played. A stern shopwalker advanced menacingly and then paused. Harry transformed the tinny notes into a haunting Irish melody. Other shoppers stopped. A small crowd formed, and the toys sold like the proverbial hotcakes. We lost Harry in his own world. He moved on to a toy piano and again filled the store with music. Harry played on misty-eyed for a few moments, then wiped his velvet sleeve across his eyes, shook his head and returned from wherever he was. 'Come on, lads he yelled' and broke into a rousing jig. Ron performed a strange sort of hornpipe, vomited into a pile of paper hats, and we fled.

The rest of the afternoon drifted pleasantly and beerily into the neon-lit evening. I have vague recollections of Soho, Raymond Revue bar and various seedy clubs, but none of the journey home until the pale dawn light saw the motley crew dropped off, shivering in the frost, back on their own doorsteps. Or in Harry's case, whichever doorstep he called his own.

We only had two days off for Christmas in those days, so it was soon back to work. That year was a hard winter, we had plenty of work to do, but most of it heavily depended on the weather. It was too cold to lay bricks because the frost affected the mortar. Laid in clay pipes, drainage system joints were formed by carefully caulking tarred hemp into the collar and forcing a mix of sand and cement around on top. It was too cold for sand and cement. Eric found us whatever work he could. We did a lot of repairs and decorations to the old farm cottages on a large country estate. However, emulsion paint was only just becoming available, and we still used a wall colouring called distemper. This had a minimal range of colours and dried to a slightly chalky texture that you could rub off with your hand.

Unfortunately, the unheated cottages let it freeze on the walls overnight, and the next morning we would have a wall coloured with a beautiful pattern of icy ferns. No matter how beautiful it looked, when it did eventually dry, it turned to powder and formed a 'dandruff' that eddied in the wind coming up through the floorboards and heaped against the skirting. Even worse was the strange material called 'ceiling white'. This was an even lower grade than distemper and seemed to comprise mainly chalky water. Over the years, they slapped coat upon coat of this on the ceiling until it built up a substantial layer and this would require scraping and washing off using a large flat distemper brush, worn too short bristles over the years. We tried washing off ceilings, ignoring the drops of icy water that ran down our arms. The water froze on the ceiling, and we resorted to scraping it off. This was picturesque but not highly effective. Ice crystals floated down, catching the shaft of light that filtered through the diamond patterns of the leaded window light. They would shimmer for a few seconds, then settle gently on the floor like snow. Unlike snow, they did not melt and unless swept up quickly turned into a sticky mush which trod everywhere.

We tried digging out trenches. This proved to be a frustrating way of keeping warm and achieving nothing. The ground was too hard to dig with a spade or fork, and an almighty swing with a pickaxe resulted in a small dent in the solid ground and an agonizing shock to the arms and shoulders. 'Right, step aside. Let the dog see the rabbit.' Ron, who demonstrated arctic trench digging. I will never know how he avoided a heart attack. Purple in the face he attacked the frozen soil with a ferocity that would have terrified a gladiator. Every time that he flagged, we would express admiration and off he would go again frantically flailing at the ground with perspiration running from his brow and his shirt steaming like a horse blanket after a hard race. Eventually, even he realized he could never class a series of small dimples as a hole. But he was not a man to give up lightly.

After brooding over a woodbine, he came up with a master plan. 'Right, bring me some old wood and rag soaked in diesel from the mixer.' He lit a fire to thaw the ground and after a few minutes stamped into the flames, scattering the ashes like a form of demented Phoenix. Ron swung his pickaxe, looking for all the world like a Viking warrior in the ruins of a ravaged, smoking, hut. It was spectacular. The top surface had melted, but only enough to form a thin, slippery layer over the iron-hard ground. His feet shot out from under him and with an unearthly shriek, he fell flat on his back. Most of the flames were out, but a sticky mess of wood ash and diesel coated him from head to toe. Only his dignity was hurt, but even then, he puffed himself up with pride when Nobby assured him that he was the only one capable of such a deed. When Eric came to pick us up that evening, he took one look at Ron and told him he was not getting into the van, and he could walk the four miles back to the village. Employment laws were quite different then.

The bad spell dragged on, and we realized that soon some of us were to be 'stood off' or sent home with no pay. The older men with a family were always the last to go - as long as there was something to do, Eric would find them something. We, youngsters, accepted our fate. This was how the industry had always been. I suppose that there must have been an unemployment pay, but we did not use it. It was a foolish person who had not saved a few weeks' wages to cover the bad time. Saving for a rainy day meant just what it said then. There were no telephones in the average home, and we would call in the yard on a motorbike if the roads were clear enough to see if there was any work going. There was usually a five-gallon drum with holes punched in the sides filled with blazing timber kept from demolition jobs. If there was no work, we often sat around the drum, making tea in a small bucket and pouring in a tin of condensed milk and a packet of sugar. This was unlike any tea I have tasted since, strong, orange and tasting of wood smoke. We made toast by the flames of the impromptu brazier and sat until kippered by the wood and tobacco smoke of our companions. Uncle told tale after tale, rocking with mirth, slapping his substantial thighs and giving an occasional cough when the combined smoke became too much for even a seasoned veteran like him. I suppose with a healthier lifestyle, he would not have died as a young ninety-seven-year-old.

This year we were only out of work for days before Eric came up trumps. One of the large country estates had a derelict barn that was no longer needed. It stood miles from anywhere at the bottom of a track. It would probably be a listed building now, but then we didn't even get planning permission. We demolished it, saving all the tiles and cleaning and stacking the bricks. This gave us a few weeks' work. The winter persisted, day after day of frost, with occasional freezing fog covering the bare branches with a rime. There was a snowfall one day. We got close to the barn but walked the last half mile or so; the snow crunching under our feet and the breath catching in our throat and burning our chests with the intense cold. It was fairyland, branches and trees coated in white and glistened against a sky of intense unsullied blue. Not a bird sang, nor an animal scurried. There was a silence that I had never experienced before. The snow muffled the sound, I know, but this was more than that. A sparkling vacuum of white crystals, a silence that I could feel and a sense that life had not changed in this valley for centuries. I felt somehow that it would be almost sacrilege to scar the peace and beauty of this spot on a day like this, strangely Eric must have felt it too.

'Too cold for work today lads, I'll pay you for the day, run you back to the transport caff, buy you idle sods a breakfast, then go where you like, I'm for the pub.' His father, old Fred, hopped from one foot to the other, speechless with rage and spluttering like a wet cat when he found out. He had never been in a pub. Nor had he ever paid for a minute's work not done. Uncle summed it up as he blew the froth from his whiskers, standing with legs slightly apart and his back to the blazing log in the inglenook of the public bar, 'Trouble with my brother, all religion, no soul see.'

20

Man's Best Friend

I parked my motorbike in the old shed and went whistling up the garden path. As I opened the door and stepped into the kitchen, a low rumbling growl greeted me. My mother was holding onto the collar of the ugliest looking bull terrier that I have ever seen. An old English bull terrier, squint and blood-shot eyes and a mangy off-white coat. 'What on earth is that?'

'This,' my mother replied, 'Is Gussie. Dad promised that we would look after him because his owner has a few problems with him'. This was to prove a master of understatement, like saying that Atilla the Hun inclined to be antisocial. In fact, come to think of it, Gussie would have made an ideal family pet for Attila.

His chief ambition in life was to fight, not just other dogs but cows, horses, tractors, and bicycles were all grist to Gussie's mill. Fortunately, he tolerated women and children; however, most men were high on his list of potential sparring partners, and he regarded me as a fair game.

For the next couple of days, we eyed each other warily and growled at each other as we passed. He enjoyed the same relationship with my father; we took turns in feeding him. This increased his enjoyment of life as he looked forward to biting the hand that fed him. He would sit on my girlfriend's knee and gaze adoringly at her while she told him how gorgeous he was. When I approached, his little slant eyes would narrow, his lips would curl back from admittedly impressive, if somewhat yellowing fangs, and he would invite me in dog language to step outside and discuss it. By this time, my father had acquired a pre-war standard car, of which he was very proud. 'What that dog needs,' he proclaimed, 'Is to get out more. Not just for walks in the country, into town. Get used to meeting people'. I had my own theory about what the dog really needed but went along with my father's idea. So, we took Gussie to town. This simple statement disguises the reality. It is like saying, 'They built the pyramids.'

First, we had to get him in the car. If he had not worn a muzzle, it would have been easier to get a crocodile into a dustbin. That dog might have seemed to have short legs, but he could brace them against opposite sides of the door and still have legs spare to scrabble frantically backwards. Finally, all three of us were in and exhausted. The dog and I sank into the back seat with me clinging onto his lead with a restraining arm locked around his muscular neck. Dad settled into the driver's seat but shook his head. 'No, I don't like this. I'm not happy with that ugly bugger breathing down my neck.' I understood. I had an interesting wrestling match with Gussie as we swapped sides, he gained great pleasure from head butting me as he attempted to tear chunks out of me, but I hoisted him on to my knee and pinned him on the opposite side of the back seat. We went about twenty feet with him struggling and protesting vocally before the car ground to a halt. 'Can't you control that animal better than that?' asked my father. 'It is only a dog.'

'It's not only a dog. It's a bloody hell hound. If you can do any better come and have a go, I'll drive.'

'Right,'

'Right,'

Two sets of doors flew open, out flew Gussie. I howled in frustration, but much to our amazement the dog hopped into the front passenger seat and sat bolt upright, looking through the windscreen with a haughty expression before turning a supercilious face to me and looking down his nose at the backseat passenger. We got the message; he was a front seat type of dog, Gussie had trained us.

He also taught us that, no, he didn't want to walk around on a lead and where other dogs might regard a lamppost as a convenience; he regarded them as an inconvenience. One for attacking and up-rooting. He reserved his deep hatred for hats. We would drive along with Gussie looking like a shortsighted dowager peering calmly through the windscreen when he would see a person wearing a hat. There would be an explosion of fang and claw, and they would reduce him to a hysterical rage. It was my ambition to take him to a wedding and watch while he had a nervous breakdown, but this was vetoed as being too cruel. One really annoying aspect was his inability to remember who had left him in the car. He took his guarding duty very seriously and sometimes would not let my father back in when he had driven Gussie. He did the same to me when I was in the car, so it made sense to meet up and approach the car together. He would rush from side to side growling fiercely before realising that we were both there and then he would sit sheepishly waggling his stump of a tail and waiting for praise.

Gussie stayed with us for several months and eventually lost the urge to tear lumps out of us, but it was obvious that he was never to be trusted. He trapped a gang of rail workers in their wooden hut and prowled around it, tearing lumps out of the woodwork for several hours. There were no mobile phones in those days, of course, and they were stuck there until his stomach told him it was teatime and he proudly trotted home again.

His downfall came when he crossed the law. We had a fence around the garden and a gate about four feet high leading out onto a quiet road. One day the village policeman came cycling slowly past, enjoying the late summer sunshine, secure knowing that nothing on his beat was amiss. Gussie's head jerked up on his short neck, and a maniacal gleam flashed from his piggy eyes. A hat. Not only that, a hat on a bicycle. Two of the things he had sworn to eradicate from decent society. His short, muscular legs propelled him down the path on his mission, and he hurtled down the path and launched himself over the gate like a champion showjumper. Our frantic calls alerted the constable, and he glanced over his shoulder. Aghast, he stood up on his pedals and prepared to accelerate up the road. Too late. Like a well-aimed missile, Gussie grabbed the rear wheel of the bike and shook it. The bike stopped dead and launched the unfortunate police officer over the handlebars. He landed in an undignified heap on the grass verge and his helmet went bowling off down the road. Gussie was in heaven. He had a general homicidal urge, but his two real enemies were available, and he chewed the tyre to shreds before reducing the helmet to tatters.

The policeman sat in our kitchen and sipped the tea. 'That there animal 'as got to go, Jack,' He was saying. 'I know you mean well, but it ain't goin' to work.' My father shook his head sadly and admitted defeat. They both rolled a cigarette from the pack of Golden Virginia, lit up and sat back to seal the fate of the dog who sat on the lawn outside coughing up lumps of rubber and blue material.

As it happened, the solution was simple. Some people would say it was cruel, but times were harder in those days. They condemned Gussie to spend the rest of his days with an elderly spinster with a walled garden and severe agoraphobia. It proved a match made in heaven. They both hated meeting people and loved eating chocolate. Gussie eventually became too fat and contented to growl at anyone, and they sat in chairs on each side of the fireplace gazing at each other fondly and farting. Amazingly, they both lived to a ripe old age despite their diet and lack of exercise.

21

Haunted

We spent a lot of time working along the Wiltshire, Hampshire, Berkshire borders. It was always an enjoyable drive through some of the finest high chalkland before dropping down into one of the ancient villages that straddled the boundary. Now most of them are occupied by people who commute to one of the larger towns, but over forty years ago, most of the villagers worked locally on one farm, racing stables or larger estates. Of course, some bigger cottages were owned by wealthy retired people who employed us to do their building work. In other cases, the larger landowners employed us to do the larger jobs that their own odd job man was too busy to do. This provided an interesting variety of work and a chance to meet many people, most of whom had time to talk to us while we worked and supply endless cups of tea.

This was in the days before supermarket shopping and this, combined with infrequent buses, meant that most of the villages had a variety of shops, not just a general store but separate butchers, bakers and of course a Post Office and several pubs. One baker, in particular, was opposite a cottage where we worked, and the smell of fresh bread tantalised us from early in the morning. By the time our ten-o'clock tea break came, we were desperate and made a beeline for the open door. There was not just bread. Every day there would be a mouthwatering selection of home-baked pies, cakes, and other goodies. Perhaps the most memorable was their Wiltshire lardy cake. For anyone not familiar with this, you have missed an experience. This was not the pale imitation that is bought now. This would probably carry a Government health warning these days. Baked to perfection with a soft golden-brown crust, the sweetened bread mix was liberally laced with currants and sultanas and folded over on itself and combined with layers of sugar and lard melted into mouth-watering layers. I felt some of you flinch when I said lard. I feel sorry for you; you have missed one of life's pleasures, maximum taste, and no guilt in those days about the thousands of calories. Some of you will have gained surplus pounds just reading about it!

For those without a sweet tooth, there was another option. The butcher cooked his own ham, the smell of which wafted along the village street and encouraged the purchase of a crusty loaf from the baker to take down for a couple of slices of succulent ham from the bone. Not thin, watery, plastic ham, but real succulent fresh cooked meat with no additives or injected preservatives. Fortunately, most of us worked hard enough to burn off the calories, and this was just as well, as there were no gyms around in those days to compensate.

As well as these tempting businesses, there were other, more practical, but especially useful concerns. Many villages boasted a blacksmith's forge. As well as shoeing horses, they made and repaired many metal items. Farm machinery was not so sophisticated then, neither were the majority of cars, and they made many ingenious repairs. They also made gates, both wrought iron and tubular field gates, and various hinges and latches. A lot of homes used solid fuel to cook on and heat the water. The 'posher' ones used Aga ranges. Law required all agricultural cottages to have a solid fuel cooker - these were usually a similar type to Aga known as Rayburns. Both types stood in a brick opening slightly larger than the range, with a mantlepiece above, allowing the lids of the hob to open. The black enamelled flue pipe from the cooker then passed through a metal plate into the chimney itself. These were known as register plates, were made of relatively thin metal and incorporated a sliding metal hatch just big enough for the chimney sweep to feed his brushes through. Most of the chimneys were large and did not have flue liners like the modern ones. When it rained a certain number of drops would patter down the opening and gather on top of the register plate. In time the plate would rust through, and that would be another little job for us.

One day I was going down to the forge in the next village to collect one of these plates. It was lunchtime and as I crossed the high ridge by Inkpen Beacon, and I pulled the van over to have my lenght break. A tall, wooden, T shaped structure that I had often seen before dominated the skyline, and I was curious. There was no one around, so I sat on the sun-warmed grass and watched a buzzard sail majestically along the ridge above a rolling landscape that seemed empty of human life. The views were magnificent. The day was pleasantly warm, and hardly a breath of air ruffled the wildflowers. Having finished my sandwich, I started up the van and wound down to the forge to pick up the plate.

I helped the blacksmith slide the plate into the van and then just as I was leaving I wound the window down and said, 'Here Sid, what's that wooden pole thing on top of the hill where I had my break?' He looked at me strangely and pushed his cap back on his forehead.

'Mean to say you don't know?' he asked incredulously. I shook my head. 'Wouldn't catch me stoppin' up there that you wouldn't. That there's Coombe Gibbett. Back along they hung people off the crossbars of that there gallows, haunted it is. Haunted.'

I tried to find out more, but Sid did not know; he was content to leave well alone and respect the fact that people had avoided it for years.

With my curiosity now thoroughly aroused, I asked around until the true story was revealed. In fact, the Gibbet was only used once, in 1676. A George Broomham was entertaining his lover, Dorothy Newman from the neighbouring village of Inkpen. Presumably, it was a warm summer's day, similar to the one I chose, and they were enjoying the outside activity when George's wife, Martha, stumbled across them. Robert, their young son, accompanied her. George was obviously a man of action, not words because he proceeded, with the help of Dorothy, to drown his wife and son in a large dew pond which was conveniently situated close by.

They chose the wrong day. It was obviously far busier than the day I decided for my lunch because the village idiot, a lad called 'barefoot mad Tom' witnessed them. Shoes or not, Tom made it back to the village and could tell a coherent enough story to be believed. Justice was short and sharp in those days. They were hauled before the Winchester court and promptly hanged. As a warning to the local wrongdoers, their corpses were hung in chains, and they swung side by side from the T piece of Coombe Gibbet. It is not recorded how long they dangled there, but it was customary to leave the bodies of criminals hanging on display for months, if not years. Environmental issues were not so pressing in the seventeenth century.

The original gibbet rotted away, but the villagers had got so used to it dominating the skyline that another was erected. It sits almost a thousand feet above sea level on the highest chalk hill in England. It has been erected on top of a massive Iron Age burial mound, the outline of which can still be seen. If you visit the site, you may not see the buzzards. Now it is used by hang glider and paragliding enthusiasts. Don't go on a warm sunny day, choose a dark night when the wind scuds drifting clouds across the moon, causing moving mysterious shadows. It is possible to park close to the gibbet. Wind the car window down enough to let the tendrils of cold mist touch your cheek, watch the scudding clouds give the illusion that the top of the gibbet is swaying and listen to the wind moaning through the cross trees. Then tell Sid it is not a haunted place.

Under a spreading chestnut-tree, the village smithy stands; The smith, a mighty man is he, with large and sinewy hands; And the muscles of his brawny arms, are strong as iron bands - Henry Wadsworth Longfellow

22

Scrumpy

For those of you who may not have come across them, dewponds are man-made ponds sited on the highest parts of the chalk downlands and reputed never to run dry. I have looked at many sources of information, and there is no end of information available on how to make dewponds, but no one seems sure why they work. With a general acceptance of dewponds dating from Neolithic times, like many incredible construction concepts spanning back thousands of years, it leaves those of us with interest in how 'planning conversations' may have sounded.

'Ok, Inken. I've got your proposal here, and it seems logical.'

'I see you propose that we go up to the highest point of the downs. This is the highest point above the nearest water supply and the furthest and most inconvenient place to carry the tools and materials, as you rightly say. OK, using our antler horn picks we dig a hole eight-foot deep into the hard chalk. Then we line this hole with clay-packed well down.

Oh, I see, only about two hundred and fifty tons of it. Shouldn't take much carrying up the thousand-foot hill then. (Hmm... Pity the wheel is yet to be invented).

Pack it all down. Grind chalk up small and mix it with water. Hmm, let's see about two thousand of those beakers should do it and only three miles to carry. Providing that it doesn't dry out and crack up as we build it. If all goes to plan, it will then hold water.

Where will this water come from then? What do you mean, you don't know?

In over two thousand years they will still argue about it, will they? Sorry, your theory doesn't hold water.

Sit down over there, close your eyes and stretch out your neck. A pleasant, kind Druid will see to you in a minute.'

This could also explain the burial mound, of course, but no matter what, someone built a dewpond, and it worked. And, in some parts of the country, we refer them to as mist ponds, in others as cloud ponds. Some authorities dismiss it out of hand and say that the ponds rely upon rainfall to keep them replenished. One thing is certain though, the ponds never dry up, even in the longest droughts. In fact, measurements show that they often achieve the highest levels of water in the driest conditions.

There were quite an industry building dewponds in the eighteenth and early nineteenth centuries and small gangs of craftsmen started in September. They worked their way around Wiltshire, Berkshire and into Sussex. However, there were small regional differences in construction. For anyone interested, I suggest that you look at The Dewpond Makers of Imber, written by the Reverend Edgar Glanfield in 1922. He was the Vicar of Imber, the 'ghost village' on Salisbury Plain from which the Army evicted the inhabitants. This derelict and deserted village, with the wind howling through the ruins, was once picturesque. Rev Glanfield mentions the names of dewpond builders who were octogenarians in 1922. The names include Charles Wise, Joel Cruse, Jabel Earley and Daniel Pearce, and all these surnames are still found within a few miles of Imber and are still connected to the construction industry. I have worked with a Charlie Wise. His ancestors came from Imber, and he is a character in his own right and also with several Pearces, all craftworkers of the old school.

When I started work over fifty years ago, I worked with some men who had started their working life sixty years before me, in the early nineteen hundreds, and the Joels and Jabels of the previous generation taught their trade. In this way, we learned many skills that only specialist conservation companies now teach. The retired workers would meet for a pint in the local, most would get dressed up to go out with shiny shoes and watch chains stretched across the serge of their waistcoats. Sitting in their favourite chair, they wrapped their wrinkled, weather-beaten hands around a pint of beer and puffed their old blackened pipes, pausing now and then to sip and then blow the froth off their walrus whiskers.

These old-timers would call the sixty-year-olds that we worked with 'boy.' I always regret that I could not tape-record the conversation and banter that took place. Here was a group of men that had lived and most times, served under Queen Victoria. The BBC or education had not corrupted their accents and dialect, and they spoke as their ancestors might have done centuries before. Sometimes, it was even possible to tell which village they originated from because of subtle variations in accent or speech pattern. The old soldiers amongst them were a direct link to the Army of Kipling's poems, and they sat talking of 'Fuzzy-wuzzies', 'Dervishes' and 'char wallahs'. They had done their bit before the slaughter of the First World War, although some as forty-year-olds, had taken part in this.

It may have been only fifty years ago, but it was a different era. For instance, there were no mechanical diggers around apart from the giant draglines used in railway and civil engineering projects. All other excavation was done by hand. To lay the main sewer in a road, a contractor would hire a gang of 'Navvies' to dig with picks and shovels, and as always where there was hard work to undertake, the Irish were highly prized.

The main drainage did not come to our group of villages until a couple of years after we moved there, so all waste disposal took place by the time-honoured method of 'bucket and chucket.' We would dig a hole in the garden and bury it, or by septic tank or cesspit. Where there was no garden, the earth closet would have a bucket and a wagon with a built-in tank collected this. We emptied the bucket into the tank, and the driver would then spread it on the fields. The villagers who had an earthy sense of irony normally referred to this wagon as the 'honey wagon'.

* * *

As you turn left at the bottom of Hurstbourne Tarrant hill, the minor road winds along the valley bottom. About a mile and a half outside of the village some wooden bungalows with corrugated roofs stood, in approximately an acre of garden. This land worked mainly as a vegetable garden with some fruit trees. It was an idyllic situation. Across the open fields opposite, the river Bourne meandered across the meadows. There would be an occasional splash and quack from the resident mallards, but little else disturbed the peace. On one particular day, there was an additional noise. It was mid-March, and an early Cuckoo was frantically advertising his services. Two elderly ladies lived in one of the bungalow's that we were carrying out some maintenance. We had given the corrugated iron roof a couple of coats of tar. Where the iron was a little thin, we cut a patch of hessian sacking and stuck it on with tar. We applied a couple of more coats of tar, and a weatherproof roof was ready for another few seasons wear, and we repaired the guttering around the roof and painted inside with bitumastic paint. All was well and going to plan, and with the work done on top, it was time to move down to ground level.

Now we were looking at the drainage. All the downpipes flowed into an underground tank, and they pumped the water with the old cast iron pump and used it for washing or watering the garden. The drinking water came from a well. This worked most of the time, but during heavy rain, the underground tank overflowed and flooded the path. Therefore, we were digging a trench from the tank into which we could lay drainage pipes into a pit filled with rubble, called a soakaway. Excess water would then run into the soakaway and eventually find its way into the watercourse.

In those days there was no plastic pipe or even couplers for the clay drains. We made each joint individually by forcing a coil of tarred hemp into the collar of the pipe and then applying a band of sand and cement known as 'pug'. The day had started cool enough. In fact, the two spinsters had brought us out a glass of sloe gin, 'Made from they blackthorn in yonder hedge, just to get 'ee goin' look.'

Now the sun that was encouraging and was warm on our bare arms and brought sweat to the brow.

'Casn't have 'ee slackin' my hansoms', said our elderly ladies.

'We got summat here to quench 'ee'. They produced a stone flagon of homemade cider. This was my first experience of 'scrumpy.' I was used to the fizzy, innocuous bottled cider. They lowered the stone flagon down the well with a piece of rope passed through the handle, and now and then we took a swig of the chilled liquid.

We finished it at lunchtime, sitting with our backs to the old apple tree and enjoying pickled onions with bread and cheese brought out to us by our benefactors.

'All frum our garden, cheese frum our goat an' all,' they beamed. I looked at Harry he could have posed for a picture called contentment.

'Sure, this is a glorious life altogether, but we have to make a start.' We got to our feet and promptly bumped into each other, attempting to steady each other. We took a couple of tentative steps and then bounced off each other again. Giggling like schoolgirls, we clutched and leaning shoulder-to-shoulder staggered toward the trench. At first, there was no sign of Ron. We squinted up and down the trench line and saw a pair of boots sticking out, one on each side. Looking down, we saw Ron, flat on his back, legs in the air. One arm was feebly circling in the air as Ron conducted an imaginary band and he wrapped the other around the stone cider flagon. With his lips pursed, we could make out the tune as he trumpeted 'Seventy-six trombones in the big parade'.

Harry and I sobered up enough to dig the soakaway. We left Ron in blissful contentment lying in the trench until Eric came to collect us that evening. The two elderly ladies were most concerned.

'Ee don't look like the sort wi' a weak constitution do 'ee? Our brother used to drink one of they flagons by 'imself when he dug the garden.'

As we drove home, Eric chuckled, 'Should have warned you, their brother died of alcohol poisoning.'

23

Brush with the Law

Again we were working in a large country house, through ivy-clad lodge gates and up a drive lined with majestic trees. This house was unoccupied, and the owners had employed a Clerk of Works to oversee operations. 'Bertie' was a small bumptious man who would leap out of his Austin Cambridge and strut across the site like a little bantam cock. He then waved his arms around and gave a string of contradictory instructions before retreating, shaking his head and clicking his tongue like a man in the grip of a strange illness. Larry was terrified of him and tried to carry out all instructions; this leads to a spiral of minor disasters and spiralling rages. Eric was an education to watch. He would calmly agree with whatever the demented bantam suggested and then do precisely what he wanted to. 'Trained by experts,' he grinned. 'How do you think we got up the beaches in Normandy?' Take all the orders and pick the sensible ones.

We noticed that 'Bertie the Bantam' had an aversion to litter and would walk out of his way to aim a kick at any cement bags or debris that lay around. Harry laid a careful trap with one empty cardboard box, and one a few feet away filled with bricks but with the lid fluttering temptingly in the wind. Sure enough, Bertie took the bait and sent the first box sailing in the air with a well-aimed kick. Two quick steps on and his immaculately polished toecap thudded into the brick filled box. Bertie howled in pain and sat nursing his ankle. He looked up at the concerned face of Harry. 'Sure, you'll be taking the creases out of those trousers sitting on the ground there. I suppose you'll be looking at that box of brick samples we put out for ye?' Bertie limped off to his car and sat there, beating his hands on the wheel for a moment. Harry returned with an innocent expression expressing indignation at the ingratitude of officialdom.

The outside of the house, covered in scaffolding, invited us, youngsters, to swing on it like a troupe of monkeys. On the lower bars, we jumped up, dangled off the tube with outstretched arms, and then swung our feet through to turn a somersault. Rightly, Ron used to tell us not to. It was only a matter of time before we talked him into showing us how it ought to be done, of course. Helped by betting him a Woodbine that he could not do it. There was very little that Ron would not do for a Woodbine.

Ron was the proud owner of a pair of extraordinary boots. He had bought these in a jumble sale, and they were old, Uncle said he thought they were Spanish Civil war boots, Eric thought they were probably Russian, Harry dismissed this theory, saying that he had never met a Russian with a sense of humour. In any event, these boots were almost as wide as they were long, a similar shape to table tennis bats but also thick and clumsy. They suited Ron well. He jumped, gripped the rail, and swung his legs through his ankles. Well, he would have done, but his boots were wider than the space between his wrists and they jammed in. Ron hung upside down, swinging in the gentle breeze like a giant sloth. 'Gi's a hand down you' he implored. We stood and discussed the merits of Nortons compared to BSA motorcycles. Ron clung on grimly, his voice becoming more agitated. 'C'MON YOU BUGGERS, GET US DOWN!' Nobby pretended to notice his predicament for the first time and extended a hand to give Ron a gentle push on the rump. Ron swung backwards and forward. When he slowed down, Nobby would give him another shove. We reduced Ron to threats and Anglo-Saxon oaths until the inevitable happened, and he dropped neatly on his head into the sand pile. It was not far to fall. He was unhurt and leapt to his feet, showering sand and insults at our rapidly disappearing backs.

We didn't spend all day playing around, of course. We spent most of the time working, usually in very agreeable surroundings. For example, we had a regular contract in an isolated village on a hilltop. One titled Lady owned the whole of the village, except for the church and vicarage. It was the closest thing to the old feudal system that I have ever seen. Apart from the vicar, everyone in the village either worked for this Lady or was married or related to someone who did. When they were too old to work, they stayed in their tied cottage until they died. Even the vicar had to 'toe the line'. If her Ladyship did not approve of the service, his church would soon be empty. She even owned the pub and had donated the village hall. There were two buses a week, one on market days and one on Saturdays. Strangely enough, all the villagers who I met seemed quite content with their lot, even if it was restrictive.

They built most of the cottages of brick and flint, meaning that the corners, or quoins as we called them, were red brick. Bands of these red bricks ran through the length of the building horizontally with in-filled panels of flintstone. Built-in the days before damp courses, her Ladyship employed us to provide one in every cottage where needed. Now there are modern ways of providing a damp course to prevent rising damp, back in the 1950s we used to insert slates. The problem was that it meant a lot of work if we disturbed the panel of flint when we cut a horizontal slot for the slate. The answer was to insert one slate at a time into the brickwork course and wait for the mortar to harden before cutting out another slot and inserting the next.

Nobby and I had a wheelbarrow, and once loaded, we pushed it from one cottage to the next, replacing one slate at a time until we reached the end of the road. Then we pushed it back up to the top and came back down, replacing the next slate. We repeated the process until the whole of the cottage had a neat band of slate right round it. This sounds boring, but in fact, it was most enjoyable. It was the first job that I was in charge of; I was eighteen, nearly earning a man's wage, and could see the results of my labour. All the cottages had enormous gardens, most of these were full of vegetables and fruit, and the grateful cottagers gave us bags of fresh produce to take home and kept us supplied with tea and homemade cake all day. One elderly lady brewed her own beer and made cider from the apples in her garden, and we learned to treat this with respect after spending one afternoon bumping into each other and giggling uncontrollably.

When bored, old Uncle used to come along for the day, he would always ask me what I wanted him to do and treat me like a proper foreman, but I had no false illusions. He had probably forgotten more than I knew. I gave him an old beer crate to sit on where he would chip away, puffing on his pipe, cackling with laughter as he chatted to the occupant. The rich, broad accents sounded almost like a foreign language as they reverted to the dialect and grammar of their youth. I felt privileged glimpsing a way of life unchanged for centuries, and people who welcomed you left their doors unlocked and shared what little they had.

Later in the year, we had a larger job, and Harry and Dick joined us. I had never met the Lady estate owner, who the villagers held in awe. I imagined a very grand person, maybe with a tiara and mink coat. We were taking out an old solid fuel cooker and replacing it with a Rayburn. These ranges, similar to an Aga, were very popular in farm cottages where there was a law requiring the landlord of agricultural cottages to provide a solid fuel means of cooking and heating. The housewife had gone to visit a friend in the village and left strict instructions with us to get two large loaves from the baker. Nearly everything was delivered then, and the baker, butcher, fishmonger, coalman and paraffin for the heaters were all delivered to the door. As we worked away, Dick treated us to a selection of his Canadian songs and Harry whistled cheerfully. The door swung open, and a grey-haired woman in a scruffy raincoat entered with a huge wicker basket over her arm.

'Top of the morning, me little Darlin, two of your large ones please.' Said, Harry.

'What?'

'Two large ones' repeated Harry, a bit slower this time. She glared at him.

'Jeez, are you may be a bit deaf?' Harry enquired? There was an explosion.

'Who the devil do you think I am, you horrible little man? I own this village, I own as far as you can see, and as long as you are on my land you and the band of brigands with you call me Madam, understood?'

Harry quailed, even his legendary charm failed against this Gorgon. Breeding showed. The genes that had made mutineers quake and sent pirates scuttling away had concentrated into this unlikely-looking Lady. We stood dumbly and rode out the tirade until she stormed regally out with a dismissive wave of her scruffy mittens.

I was to meet this formidable person again, and once more, she held all the trump cards. One of my friends had his eighteenth birthday party and so could legally drink in our 'local'. We had a couple of pints and took some beer back for an impromptu party. As far as I know, there was no lager not in this pub. Beer either came out of a barrel and they pumped it manually from the cellar, or in bottles.

If you bought bottled beer, the bottles were returnable, and there was a small amount repaid on each one. We bought a couple of wooden crates of beer, one of brown ale and one of Bass. The two wooden crates containing glass bottles full of beer were quite heavy, so three of us carried them off down the village street—one in the middle using both hands and one on each side using either his left or right. There was no problem walking three abreast down the road. Cars were few and far between. There were no street lamps, so we could see one coming by its headlights, even before we heard it.

After a couple of hundred yards, we saw some lights coming and piled onto the pavement. The old Austin juddered to a halt, and the window wound down to reveal another mate of ours. 'What's on then?'

'We're having a bit of a party, Pete. Fancy joining in?'

'Too true I do, tell you what I'll give you a lift.'

We humped the crates over to the car and looked inside. Not for nothing did they call these 'Baby Austins' - if they carried four passengers, they needed to be quite friendly. This one had five in it.

'Forget it, mate, we'll walk.' I said.

'Don't be daft, two of you stand on the running boards, rest the crates on the bonnet and hang on to them, and Chris can sit on the luggage rack on the back', came the reply.

Looking similar to one of those cars in which clowns enter the circus big top, we weaved off down the road. It was about a mile, and we were travelling at around ten miles-an-hour, I suppose. Only one other car overtook us, a young couple who passed with a toot and wave. Then disaster struck. The solid figure of our local constable stepped out of the shadows and waved us to a halt. We greeted him cheerfully enough, expecting to receive a telling off. He held a finger to his lips and nodded at the hedge. There was his sergeant carefully leaning his bicycle against a tree. 'Good job I'm doing my rounds 'ey constable?' Thought you said there would be no trouble tonight?'

That man deserved promotion to Chief Inspector as he subsequently was many years later. The charge sheet made it look as if he had cleared up a crime wave and broken up a gang of desperate criminals. Charged only with aiding and abetting the carriage of goods dangerously, I got off lightly. However, he charged all five of the car passengers, and us three villains clinging to the outside of the car with something. He must have combed the statute books for obscure mediaeval laws. We presented ourselves at court, suits pressed, hair combed and faces shining with soap. There on the bench as presiding Magistrate was Lady B. No longer was she in a scruffy old coat, now she sat in all her finery and glowered at us. She recognised me immediately as one peasant who had mistaken her for a mere tradesperson, and her eyes glinted with pleasure. I swear that she reached under the bench for a black cap to put on her head before proclaiming the death sentence, but in the end, she had to settle for the maximum fine that the law allowed, so it cost me a good week's wages. She pronounced with pleasure, 'This sort of offence is becoming far too common,' but even our local police officer couldn't think of another one in the county.

* * *

I must say that our local constable's idea of the law didn't always follow the conventional path. For instance, he once approached a group of youths who were sitting on motorcycles in the small square outside the village shop. They were talking, laughing, and smoking the odd cigarette, no one including the constable minded. 'I know where they are,' we heard him remark. We treated him with friendly respect. He helped run the youth club and played cricket with some lad's fathers. Inevitably, one motorcyclist didn't conform. He sat defiantly, astride his bike as the law approached. 'Do me a favour, get some tax on that bike when you get your wages', said the constable, nodding amiably at the rest of us before sauntering off. The next Saturday the scenario repeated itself with more of direction. 'I'm not telling you again, sunshine, tax that bloody bike or it will cost you money.' Some people never learn. And the same situation repeated the following week. This time the police officer looked in amazement at the expired tax disc and strode purposefully forward. The policemen carried a large wooden truncheon in a pocket that ran down the outside of their leg. He drew this truncheon and with the same swing that scored sixes on the cricket field beat in the glass on the motorcycle headlight. 'Told you it would cost money, see you next week.'

The following week he nodded in approval at the fresh tax disc in its holder and the brand-new headlight glass. Some years later there was a lad with a very fast bike which he rode well, but far too quickly. It was only a matter of time before the inevitable happened and one evening we heard the distinctive roar of this bike followed by a screech of tyres and a crunch. The total silence afterwards was the unnerving part. I rushed out. There was a mangled heap of twisted metal, blood everywhere, and assorted body parts scattered along the road. Unless Steve the rider had been wearing a fur coat, none of them belonged to him though, and there was no sign of a motorcyclist. A small crowd had gathered by now, and we heard a faint moan from the river. It became clear what had happened. A deer had jumped out in the road and was hit by the speeding bike. Steve carried on at the same speed without his motorcycle. He sailed through the air, clearing the small stream that ran alongside the road, only to plunge into the reeds and marshy ground on the other side. He was lucky, and there was nothing that a couple of weeks in hospital and a few months on crutches wouldn't cure and we received a full report of the interview in hospital conducted by our 'copper'. According to old Jim, who was in the next bed, it went something like this.

"And what sort of speed were you doing.'

'Dunno, 'bout ninety I suppose,'

'I see,' said the policeman, writing 'approximately forty miles an hour.'

'No, no, at least eighty,' said Steve.

'That's what I've got. You were doing forty. The deer was doing forty. No chance of either of you stopping, head-on, speed of eighty, pure accident.' He closed his notebook.

'You are insured, aren't you, Steve?' Steve nodded mournfully.

'Yeah' third party only though and the bike's a writeoff. Still, I wanted a bigger one anyway,'

'A bigger one? Blimey, what are you after next? A Moose?' Responded the upholder of law and order.

Some villagers complained, saying Steve deserved to be prosecuted, but it was all explained in the pub after a cricket match. 'Look, this is how I see it. The lad has lost a couple of months' wages. He won't get any money off the insurance, so he has lost the price of his bike, and all his mates are calling him Moses since they dragged him out of bullrushes. Besides, he only damaged the front of the deer.'

'What has that got to do with it?' inquired the landlord. Our police officer grinned.

'Best part to eat, the rear haunch and saddle of venison.' Stan, the landlord, shook his head in amazement. The evidence had formed part of the menu at the police house.

The system worked for this enlightened lawman; it was not just that he hated paperwork, although that was probably part of it. By his reasoning everyone gained, his patch was statistically low on recorded crime, local lads avoided a criminal record, and he had the support of the entire community who knew that he would not tolerate major crimes.

If there were no bad people, there would be no good lawyers - Charles Dickens.
The Old Curiosity Shop

24

The Missing Salmon

I t was a beautiful morning. The trees were still budding, and although the leaves were yet to flourish, the rooks could sense that spring was on the way. They circled the elms in an agitated fashion, unsure if their job was to be gathering twigs or impressing the opposite sex. Harry was leaning over the old mossy wall that surrounded the pigsty, and I could hear the contented grunting of the overweight occupant. Harry scratched between her shoulder blades with a short stick.

We were at the rear entrance to the manor house belonging to Lady B - oppressor of the peasantry and absentee Landlord. Actually, she was only absent to attend court, again. Harry was still smarting under her reprimand, and sympathising with me over my unfortunate encounter with her. Much to her disgust, she had found that I could not be transported to the colonies, and the maximum fine that she could impose was five pounds. Ironically, she was now paying me. Still, her money was as good as any other, and we had a job to do. So, we wheeled the tools down to the gatehouse where we were re-pointing the brickwork. Harry was never in a grim mood for long, and it wasn't long before he was whistling cheerfully as he worked, enjoying the warmth reflected from the mellow old bricks.

We heard the click of the gate latch and looked up as the postman leant his bicycle against the wall and sauntered up the path to push a letter through the box. 'What in the name of all the saints have you got sticking out of your bag?' asked Harry.

'What this? It's a salmon, fresh from Scotland for her Ladyship' replied the 'postie' producing an enormous parcel with the shape of a tail just discernable through the layers of hessian and brown paper.

'Don't tell me they are posting fish now' said Harry.

'Well, sort of' came the reply.

'It came on the train, and Jim asked me to drop it in. You know how it is, anything to please her Ladyship.' Harry nodded, and an angelic smile lit up his face.

'Would you like a cup of coffee? The little Darlin' who works here has just made one.' The postman looked at his watch 'Don't be worrying about the time when the good Lord made time, he made plenty of it.' said Harry. 'Sure, that's a fine fish, I haven't seen a fresh salmon since I left home. The English think it comes in tins.' This was almost true, there was no farmed salmon in those days, and many people had never seen a fresh salmon, don't forget there were no supermarkets either and a salmon like this was a luxury.

'Tell you what,' said Harry. 'You have a cup of coffee, and I will drop this down to cook.' He gave the postman a nudge and a wink. 'It'll get me in her good books too if you follow my drift.' The postman grinned, and gratefully sat down, rolling a cigarette with tobacco from Harry's battered old tin, while the new delivery man wobbled off on the bicycle.

Harry was in a good mood all afternoon and chuckled away to himself between snatches of songs. As we cleared up, I asked him how he had got on with cook.

'Fine, just fine we are off to the pictures on Saturday. By the way, don't go mentioning salmon to her.'

'Why? Didn't she like it?' I asked.

'She didn't get it. That old divil she works for doesn't deserve a fine fish like that. I decided it would be pearls before swine, and that gave me the idea. The ould sow in the sty would appreciate it more than the other rich sow, and that is where it went, me boyo.'

About this time, my girlfriend's family moved to Dorset. They had previously lived a couple of stops down the railway line from me in

Stockbridge. The station was like a relic from Dickensian England and still had gas lamps on the platform, which gave an unearthly effect when the mists from the river Test swirled across the station and mingled with the smoke and steam from the trains. The farm where I lived with my parents was situated just above where the river Anton joins the Test, and in the days before Dr Beeching closed many rural lines, it was a short walk down to my local station. We first met on the train, I was working close to the railway station, and my motorbike was off the road for repairs so the first morning we shared a carriage by accident. The second morning was deliberate, and the third morning I had to sprint down the platform to find the right carriage. Some rolling stock was old; this carriage was ancient. Leather straps raised and lowered the windows. There was a wooden step running alongside the coach and a large tee shaped brass door handle to twist to open the door.

I twisted and pulled. Nothing happened, I pulled harder, still nothing. The wooden door had dropped slightly and was jammed shut. There was an impatient toot from the stationmaster's whistle, but I would not admit defeat, I placed a foot on the side of the carriage and yanked on the handle with all my strength. Success! The door swung open with me clinging on the handle, and both feet clear of the floor. The sudden shock and extra weight were too much for the screws holding the hinges. They pulled out of the frame, and the door toppled over on top of me, leaving me flat on my back on the platform floor, gazing up through the open window in astonishment. Now it would be possible to sue. Then I was bundled into the carriage and sat dazed and embarrassed while they berated me and the door was screwed back on by Alf, the man who had sold me the dodgy motorbike.

Anyway, this had proved quite an effective introduction, and we continued to see each other when I went back to using the bike, partly because the next job was out of town and partly because in my experience it was safer on a motorbike than in a train. Shortly after Mary moved to Dorset, I was spending every weekend down there, and this was another reason for me buying the Triumph that I mentioned before. During the summer it was fine, and the trip of thirty-odd miles took thirty minutes once I had got passed Salisbury and onto the deserted road that swept across the undulating grassy hills to Blandford. On a winter night, it was a nightmare of icy roads that never saw a gritting lorry, so I fitted the bike with a little single-seat sports sidecar that at least meant I could skid without falling off. The sidecar had a rudimentary hood which kept some weather off the occupant. I realized how little it kept off after Mary had spent the weekend at my parents' house. My mother had sent some eggs back as a gift for my future mother-in-law, and Mary had these on her lap as she sat in the sidecar. It rained all the way down. I was ok, with a full set of waterproof clothing, but when we arrived, I opened the hood to reveal Mary sitting with an uncooked omelette in paper mache swishing about in her lap.

Suffice to say that I bought a car. However, I would not give in without a struggle. I wanted something different. Something different is what I got; I found a Morgan Super Sport for sale in a magazine. To be precise, I found a dealer called Mercury motors in Wimbledon with several Morgans for sale and rode up on the Triumph one weekend with John, a friend of mine. I went into the showroom, and there it was. A bright red three-wheeler with a massive J.A.P. twin-engine and two chrome exhaust pipes running the length of the car on the outside. 'This, sir' said the salesman, 'is, of course, the model that held the world speed record for three-wheelers of over one hundred miles, in one hour from a standing start.' I was smitten. I didn't need any sales talk. We agreed a part exchange price on my motorbike, I gave him a bundle of notes, and we roared off.

It was fast; I give him that. This was in 1959, and they had built the car in 1932, so for its age, it was remarkably fast. It had a few drawbacks. For instance, the foot brake worked on the two front wheels and the handbrake on the rear wheel, no wonder it had done one hundred miles in one hour, the driver was probably braking like mad for the last fifty miles. Not that this was too much of a problem; it was starting it that took the time.

There was no starter, and it had to be swung by hand with a starting handle. I thought the old cement mixers were bad to start, but this was a whole new experience. The engine was a high performance, high compression twin, and the mixture and advance lever had to be set just right, or it would 'kickback' violently and try to break your wrist. I learnt to swing with both hands and then brace myself. If there was a kickback and I was gripping the starting handle tightly enough, the car would leap in the air. The front wheels would lift a couple of inches off the ground before the car slammed back down. Small children formed a crowd in anticipation.

There was also no reverse gear fitted to this model, so reversing meant getting out and pushing it. It was not possible to push it with the handbrake on, of course, so this was quite an art if there was no passenger. If the ground sloped backwards, it would run away from you. If it sloped forwards, it would run away from you. Fine, if that was the way you wanted to go, but if someone had parked up close to the front on a downhill slope, it was interesting. I'd get out of the car, release the handbrake, strain like mad and push the car back. Leaning backwards with both hands gripping the car, my feet would scrabble for grip whilst I leant into the car and put the handbrake on. But if I released my grip, the car rolled forward. So, checkmate. I'd stay there until help arrived or exhaustion forced me to let go, and it rolled forward into the car in front.

Why not open the door and push with the door open? I hear you say? Silly me, I forgot to mention was no doors! Getting in required leaping over the side like jumping into a tin bath. BUT, once in with the engine throbbing away, it was a different world. There were two small screens in front and a roll of padded leather running around the cockpit. And the cockpit is what it is. Suddenly you are a fighter ace awaiting take-off, and I forgave all the faults. Well, if you are a man, the faults are forgiven. If you are wearing skirts, it is different. Did I mention that the exhaust pipes ran down the outside of the car? In fact, they were just below elbow level and carefully designed to brand the inner thigh of any unsuspecting female or kilt-clad Scott. Mary hated this car with an abiding passion that has lasted longer than the scars, so I sold it again quickly.

This was in the days before the M.O.T. test was introduced, so I bought a series of old cars to bodge up and resell. It kept me busy in the evening and provided cheap, if not very stylish motoring until I made enough money to buy a Triumph sports car. These cars were pre-war, and most of them were well past their prime. They all had idiosyncrasies. I noticed that one used to backfire a lot. I encouraged this by turning the ignition off and on as I drove the car, leading to a sound like a gunshot. One day I was driving along with a car full of mates when a herd of cows being driven home for milking, in the evening, stopped us. I pulled over tight to the verge to prevent any cows squeezing past between the car and the hedge, and the cows ambled past, swishing their tails and rolling their eyes as if they had never seen a car before. Cows are large and heavy animals with a strong desire to push each other out of the way and jostle like school children. When nearly a ton of cow bumps against a car it gives quite a jolt and I became increasingly annoyed as several tried to pass at the same time and barged along shoulder to shoulder rocking the car. I was on the verge of selling the car and did not want any damage, so hit on a brilliant idea to keep them away. I quickly turned the ignition on and off with the engine running and my foot flat on the accelerator. There was a loud report followed by total mayhem. Far from keeping them away, the herd all tried to charge through the gap at the same time.

On the old pre-war cars, there were running boards along the bottom of the doors which provided a flat platform filling in space between the front and rear 'wings', or mudguards, which stood out from the bodywork. On top of the wings were big chrome-plated headlights. Attached to the door pillars were oblong metal boxes containing indicator arms, like little flags that swung out of their containers to show which way the car was going to turn. This old Vauxhall used to look like this. Now it had a panic-stricken cow with one front and one rear leg on the ground and the matching pair on the opposite side stamping up and down on the running board until it collapsed in a mangled heap on the road. The indicator was several hundred yards up the road, accelerating faster than it had ever done before on the horns of another cow, and the headlight had been ripped off its stalk and dangled like some hideously damaged eyeball from a bunch of wires. To add insult to injury, any animal not actively engaged in wrecking the car had defecated on the windscreen and bonnet. It was several weeks before I sold this car.

25

Gamekeepers and Poachers

Before winter set in, we used to supplement our income where we could. One way was by beating. This involved driving pheasants down to the waiting guns. We would meet in the morning and take instructions from the head keeper. The under keepers and beaters would then hop onto the back of a trailer, and they would take us to the first 'drive.' This could be across fields or maybe through a wood. We spread out to form a line and making a selection of noises, rattling sticks and whistling, we walked toward the waiting guns, driving the pheasants forward. It was always an enjoyable day, and on a sunny frosty morning with the last of the leaves a golden brown and the unspoilt countryside around, I would have done it without pay. Not that the pay was good, but it was a little extra for an enjoyable Saturday when we would have only been spending money instead of earning it. We always received a bottle of beer at midday supplied by the 'Guns,' as we called the sportsmen.

Sir Bernard-Docker owned one shoot that everyone was keen to go on, a wealthy industrialist who laid on a sit-down lunch for the beaters, served in a barn and normally consisting of Irish Stew which we ate seated on hay bales. There was a strict hierarchy amongst the gamekeepers. The beaters were definitely bottom of the heap, but we enjoyed watching the jostling for position and the discussion about whose employer was top dog. Money did not count; it was all down to titles and rank. Unfortunately, neither money nor rank made a good shot, and we watched the keepers getting hot under their collars as their employers sometimes missed easy shots. One day a pheasant sailed majestically down the line of guns, who took it in turns to fire as the bird passed by. It reached the last guest who was a member of the Royal Family. He stepped smartly forward, raised his gun and fired into the air. There was a moment's silence, and then his loader, who was obviously on very easy terms with him enquired, 'What 'appened there then, sir?'

'Sorry,' came the reply. 'It was a twenty-one-gun salute, wasn't it?'

They would meticulously record each days 'bag,' and only game was supposed to be shot, but in the heat of the moment, rabbits could be mistaken for hares and the odd pigeon shot by mistake. Solemnly entering it into the Game Book, a keeper would raise a disdainful eyebrow. And to add to the 'fun', we were over the moon when we found a dead robin, or the like, and smuggled it into the game-cart. It was duly recorded by a keeper who looked as if he had just swallowed a wasp.

One of the regular beaters was a man we called Jinx. He was a tall, cadaverous figure with a long lugubrious face and a permanently worried look on his face. Jinx had been a valet in his youth and had kept many speech patterns from those days. For instance, instead of answering a query with a simple, 'Yes,' he would say, 'One would imagine so.' This became a real catchphrase for us and was employed on many building sites to the total bafflement of strangers. We used to go rough shooting ourselves when we could, and the resulting pigeons and rabbits all helped to make a bit of money and added a bit of meat to the table. Inevitably, a bit of poaching went on, nothing very sophisticated. A small group used to take a couple of air rifles out at night and spot the silhouette of a pheasant against the night sky. If they shone a light on the bird, it would not fly but craned its neck down the beam. Crack went the gun, and the bird would join his unfortunate fellows in a sack. Jinx loved the excitement of this illegal activity but as his name would suggest something always went wrong when involved.

One evening keepers disturbed them and made a run for it across a ploughed field. It was tough going across the sticky furrows, but Jinx easily outran his panting companions. They met up in a pub car park sometime later, and one of them commented on the amazing turn of speed that Jinx had shown across the clinging clay. He looked at them in amazement. 'Can't understand you, chaps. Why didn't you come on the footpath and run with me? Better than stumbling across that field.' He disappeared up the lane, being beaten with a bag of pheasants.

Jinx was an unusual man. His voice was deep and vibrant. He made an imposing figure and normally wore a tweed jacket and tie, even when he came to help us out on a building site. This meant that he was inevitably mistaken for someone of importance and being a naturally kind man, he didn't want to dissolution anyone. This led to many mistakes. Lorry drivers would happily unload the wrong materials on the wrong site, feeling totally reassured by the distinguished figure. And many a client went away convinced that the most important architect in the south of England had just given them his undivided attention.

I have never met a man with a greater talent for causing unwitting amusement. We all went cod fishing one winter and booked a boat. The excitement mounted, and we passed tips backwards and forwards about the correct tackle to use and the best bait. Jinx bought a book on fish recipes and regaled us with dozens of ways to cook cod. We set off well before daybreak and headed off to the waiting fishing boat in an old van belonging to the firm. Jinx was an expert on cod recipes by now and had our mouths watering with his descriptions. He was a talented cook and had made a huge flask of homemade soup. Every mile or so he would hold this aloft and say in his melodious voice, 'OK chaps, soon be out at sea catching cod with hot soup inside us'. When we arrived, the skipper shook his head and said that the sea was far too rough, and the wind was increasing by the minute. There was a bit of muttering and a few complaints, but we fished off the sea wall rather than waste the trip completely. The sky was the colour of lead and gusts of wind drove sheets of seawater across the harbour wall and breakwater.

We all 'tackled up' and cast in. All except Jinx, of course. He carefully laid all his tackle out in a neat line on the wall in front of him and produced his flask and a bottle of malt whisky. 'Who's for soup and a dram,' he cried, rubbing his hands together and leaping from one foot to another in anticipation.

There was an almighty crash, and a massive wave broke over the sea wall. We all got slightly wet, but it caught Jinx on one foot and sat him on his backside. He watched all his tackle, flask of soup and a bottle of whisky go bobbing out to sea. A lesser man would have shown anger. He just stood up, shook himself, then produced a soggy book of 'How to Cook Cod' from his pocket and hurled it into the water.

* * *

I passed my driving test a few weeks after my seventeenth birthday. I was used to driving a tractor around the fields and an old pickup truck along the farm tracks at home and could drive at a young age. I was told that there was a long waiting list for the driving test and the best idea was to apply well in advance, so I applied for my test at the same time that I applied for my provisional license. Much to my surprise, I was allocated a cancellation and booked a few lessons with an instructor. I treated the test as a practice and flew around the route without trying too hard. No one was more surprised than me when I passed. The driving instructor sat in his little grey Morris Minor, shaking his head in astonishment. Luckily, I had quite a lot of experience driving tractors and the old farm pickup truck, so backing and parking in tight places came easy, although my road experience was limited. Fortunately, I could answer all the questions that the examiner posed. There was no theory test in those days you just sat in the car, proved that you could read a number plate at 25 yards, and answered a few questions.

I could not really afford a car, of course, and I was still keen on motor-cycling, but few of the men could drive, and it suited Eric to have another driver at work. As well as the Minibus he had a couple of vans and an old pre-war Rover car. He entrusted me with the old car one day, and I set off to pick up another couple of workers. I left the village and spotted a soldier in uniform with his thumb held up for a 'lift'. This was quite common, national service was still running, and we all had sympathy with those who had been 'called up' to do their bit for the country. This was no youth, though. He proved to be a seasoned veteran of twenty-five or so, who pushed his maroon paratrooper's beret onto the back of his head and heaved a huge kit bag onto his lap. These kit bags were half as tall as a man and half as round but weighed nearly as much.

Pleased with the ride, he sat with it on his lap and wrapped an arm around it as if it was his girlfriend. We drove for a mile or so. He undid his collar, lit a cigarette and slouched back in his seat, a picture of contentment as he puffed away and told me tales of Suez and Malaya. I was envious and impressed as he told me of jumping into the darkness into unknown deserts and escaping the ambushes of terrorists in steamy jungles, and I realised what a sheltered, safe life I led. I pulled up at a crossroads and went to pull away. The clutch on the old Rover was unpredictable, and nothing happened for a moment, then the car gave a leap and shot over the crossroads like a startled hare. The combined weight of man and kit bag was too much for the rusty floor of the old Rover. The seat mountings tore out, tipping him backwards, and the back-seat rabbit-chopped him in the neck. For a few seconds, I thought he was dead as he lay on his back like a dead beetle. When he came round, he had lost all of his tropical tan and most of his confidence. He spent the rest of the journey on the back seat clinging on with white knuckles to the armrests. I thought he had asked to go to Newbury, but he got out at the next village, and I left him sitting on his kit bag attempting to light a bent cigarette.

I picked up Harry, and we chugged on to the large country house where we were working. It was a beautiful morning with the sun faintly peering through the morning mist. We swung through the stone piers of the driveway, and the tyres softly crunched the gravel of the winding drive. Rabbits bolted for cover up the grassy banks, their little white 'scutts' bobbing about among the drifts of yellow cowslips. So, I knew that we were the first to arrive. As normal, we unscrewed the top of our flasks and poured a cup of tea. It was warm enough to wind the window down, and we sat listening to the wood pigeons. Harry always said that they spoke to him, 'Listen' he insisted, and it was true they seemed to say, 'Take two coos, Harry, take two coos'.

The driveway must have been about a quarter of a mile long, and azaleas and rhododendrons flanked it. The azaleas were the old yellow variety that is too big for most modern gardens, and the scent was almost overpowering. I thought again how fortunate I was to earn a living in glorious surroundings and enjoy a laugh and joke with companions who felt the same way.

I consider it the best part of an education to have been born and brought up in the country - Amos Bronson Alcott

26

Worse Things Happen at Sea

Although I was the youngest, I was the only one with a driving licence, so as usual, I was at the wheel of the old Bedford van. Harry was seated next to me on the warm engine cover. Ron was sprawled in the passenger seat with his legs out, and his feet were resting on the dashboard, with his ancient hobnail boots performing an involuntary tapdance on the windscreen every time we hit a rough bit of road. This was quite often because the winter had not improved the already potholed lane that we were winding down.

Harry was in one of his poetic moods. The early spring sunshine brought out the bard in him. 'Sure, isn't it great, that Wordsworth fella? He had something. You go through winter into February. There you are, the sky the colour of an old dishcloth, hedges the colour of rabbit droppings, an' a lazy wind that would sooner go through a man than 'round him, then suddenly, you blink. And it's March. Would you just look at those daffodils, did you ever see a prettier sight?'

Ron grunted, 'Last week you was saying the same about snowdrops, you want to make your mind up, you do.'

Harry was not to be discouraged. "Snowdrops are great, but the way I see it they are like a group of shy little school girls waiting patiently to get into infant school. These daffodils now, they are like teenagers impatient to get into a dance hall, bright colours, breeze bobbing their pretty little heads.

Sure, it makes a man want to be a boy again.'

I looked across at him for a moment. He sat with a beatific smile on his face, hands crossed over his pot belly, only the red veins on his nose spoiled the cherubic image.

I recalled what Mavis the housemaid at the manor had said about him. 'Face of a cherub, mind like a midden.' Then she had smiled, 'Lovely man though for all that.'

Harry caught me looking. 'Don't get me wrong. Roses are more my choice...'

'What? The sort that grow wild in hedges?' I interrupted.

'Now there's a thought,' he said. But I was t'inking more of the late summer ones, massive great blooms hanging over a man, tempting him to gather rosebuds while he may. Lying back, drowning in fragrant petals.'

I laughed 'You're in danger of letting your memories muddle your metaphors if you don't stop there,' I said.

Ron glared at us. 'You don't 'alf talk a load of twaddle you two, what's memories got to do with the weather?'

We bickered on amiably for a mile or two while we sorted out the difference between 'metawatsits' and 'metarolgy'. Ron eventually lapsed into a sullen, confused silence under the surreal guidance of Harry and went back to examining the creased sheet of paper that was given to us by Fred as we left the Yard that morning.

To put him in a better mood, we let him play at being foreman. Not that we had much choice. He had the directions, and he was hanging onto them like a bulldog to a bull's haunch. 'Bout a mile further on you come to some crossroads, go straight over an' it's the second house on the left.'

'So, what's the address?' I enquired.

'Dunno,' he replied. 'Don't matter any' ow, got it all writ down, proper little map what Fred done.'

I approached the crossroads cautiously. There was no sign indicating who had the right of way. In fact, there were no signs at all. We crossed straight over, past a large house that lay back off the road and swung up the next gravel drive to a square brick and flint house with a slate roof. There was no sign of life as we parked on the gravel in front of the house. But this didn't matter. We had full instructions written. There was no need to get into the house as long as we had water. A quick look around confirmed that the water butts at the back of the cottage were both full. So that was another problem solved. We were here today to render the chimney breast in the roof space, that is to coat it with a smooth covering of sand, lime, and cement. In those days, the inside of the flue was not lined as it is now - usually, they were given a rough coat on the inside by leaning in and coating up inside the chimney as they built it. They referred to this as parging. With the chimney not parged, the joints in the brickwork could crumble, allowing smoke and even sparks to fill the roof space. Not wishing to increase the workload of Hampshire Fire Brigade, the owner had decided to put things right.

We unloaded the tools and materials from the van and untied the ladders from the roof-rack. The plan was to remove enough slates to let me worm into the roof space with a hurricane lamp. Harry would carry buckets up and down the ladder, and Ron would mix the mortar, 'knocking up' as it was known. The buckets would be passed through to me, and I would render the brickwork. I did not flatter myself. If the access had been easier, Ron would have been doing the rendering.

We quickly removed a patch of slates about a yard square. The roof underneath was close-boarded - they were covered in boards similar to floorboards, making life more difficult. However, Ron produced a saw, making a hole for me to crawl through. I was pleased that the loft was boarded, so I did not have to balance on the ceiling joists but could work off a flat floor. All set to go now, there was a neat pile of slates and timber at the foot of the ladder, and it was only ten o'clock, so we stopped for a tea break as normal.

It was a classic early spring day. The sky was that pure brilliant blue that you only get when there is no haze, and the gently scudding clouds were pure white, freshly laundered feather pillows. The sun was just beginning to give enough heat to show the promise that we would need to 'remove a clout' before May was in, let alone out.

Tea break over, I climbed the ladder and swung myself up into the roof space. Harry had no sooner passed the bucket of mortar through to me when I heard the scrunch of tyres on the gravel drive. There was a moment's silence and then a mounting crescendo of raised voices. Ron had strutted forward in his best 'leave it all to me. I'm in charge' mode. He was met with a moment of stunned silence before the retired Naval Commander who owned the house had unleashed a broadside. From my vantage point in the crow's nest, I could see Ron frantically waving his piece of paper like a flag of truce.

The outraged Commander leapt from one foot to another, purple in the face and verging on apoplexy. It took some time for the water to settle, but in the end, we gathered that we were in fact at the wrong house. Fred missed the large house that lay back from the road, and we were supposed to be working at the third house over the crossroads. Not the second as our drawing showed. Harry worked his charm on the commander's wife while Ron and I sheepishly restored the roof to normal. By the time we had cleared up and loaded everything back on the van, Harry and the ancient mariner were amiably seated around the kitchen table, and a large mug of coffee was waiting for us. 'Never mind, my boy,' was the commander's parting shot. 'Worse things happen at sea.' This became the standard saying whenever anything went wrong after that.

27

Sparrer Catching

On a Saturday morning, we often worked locally and finished up little odd jobs. One morning Ron and I were repairing broken slates on the roof of a cowshed. The process had not changed for centuries and armed with a slate rip. We set about the roof. The slate rip is a flat blade with a broad arrow-shaped head that we slid under a slate and drew back until a securing nail caught behind one of the 'barbs' in the head, and which point we drew it out with a sharp jerk. With the broken slates removed and the wooden battens exposed, we nailed strips of lead about three-quarters of an inch wide and six inches long to the batten, or lath as they call it in some areas. The new slate is then slid under the one above and pushed until level with its neighbours. The lead is bent up and over, to prevent it from sliding back down. Although it's not rocket science, it works well - the slates we replaced over fifty years ago are still there today.

To reach the broken slates we had two ladders. We leant one up to the eaves and the other, with a bag of straw tied to it, would be pushed up the roof and then jammed over the first ladder to secure it. (Don't try this at home, boys and girls.) With a nail hammered into the fascia, and if we secure a rope around the whole setup, it was safe. The keyword here is 'if'. Most 'gangs' just sent one worker up on the roof, while the other worker footed the ladder that leant against the eaves. We were no exception. I was in a hurry to get to my girlfriend and Ron would do anything, if told that only a brave man could do it. So, on this damp morning, Ron was up on the roof spread-eagled across the ladder, and I was footing the bottom. The barns formed a quadrangle which contained young steers, and the steers gathered around watching us with fascination. They would jostle each other, and then one adventurous animal would flick out his tongue and try to lick me. Only when a bullock has licked you, you will know the sensation. Their tongue is not soft and smooth; it is like being slapped with a warm, slimy, very scaly fish. They have an obsession with licking and have licked the enamel paint off a tractor bonnet.

I was getting increasingly irritated, and Ron called down, 'Just ignore them, don't know why you're getting your dander up 'bout a couple of licks.' 'OK!' I retorted.

'You come down here, and I'll get on the roof, you've been faffing about up there long enough, anyway.'

After a bit of argy-bargy, we swapped places. Determined to follow the advice he'd given me, Ron remained silent as the herd of aggravating adolescents pushed in closer. Then there was an almighty roar from Ron. He had been pointedly ignoring an animal that was licking the sleeve of his old coat, and the bullock had clenched his teeth on the material, and with a massive head swing had torn the sleeve from the shoulder. 'Just ignore them, Ron,' I called down. Ron freaked out and tore across the yard, arms and loose sleeve flapping like a scarecrow in pursuit of the bullocks who were enjoying this new game. I was rocking with laughter until I realized that I was sliding down the roof as the two ladders, with no one at the bottom to give weight, pushed away from the eaves. I scrabbled at the damp slates, but it was useless, and eventually, I slid down the roof and hung for a second from the rusty old cast iron gutter before it broke and deposited me into the stockyard below. In picture books, these yards are full of golden sweet-smelling straw.

In reality, the farmer did not change the straw until he turned the beasts out into the fields. A thin layer of straw was forked on top of, well, on top of whatever was there. This resulted in a thick, evil-smelling mattress that broke my fall. I lay on my back and looked up at Ron. He looked down, and his expression changed, there was no concern, it changed from delight to a smile. The smile became laughter and then howls of delight. For the first time in his life, he had come out of the situation better off than someone else. After a few seconds, I saw the funny side too, and Ron lead me over to the cattle trough and scrubbed me down with a yard broom. He wrung every bit of pleasure that he could from the situation and described to our workmates how I had rolled screaming down the roof before diving headfirst into a manure heap. Not at all like my controlled, elegant descent.

Out towards the Wiltshire border lie the series of villages known as the Chutes, Upper Chute, Chute Standen and Chute Forest among them. It is easy to get lost in the winding lanes and minor country roads that have changed very little since they were first surfaced, in most cases, just after the second world war. I always enjoyed working there, even the drive to work was a pleasure, the hedges in early summer were a mass of wild dog roses, and the cow parsley overhung the verge and brushed against the passing van releasing that strong sweet scent that always evokes summer. In the winter, if a single snowflake is seen, head for home, fast. A light covering of snow in the valley bottoms around can mean a foot of snow in Chute. We were working at an old thatched cottage that lay halfway up a hill. I can't remember which of the Chutes it was in, but I know that it was called Rose Cottage and the elderly owner was very sociable.

I always asked about local history wherever I was working, but on this occasion, she shook her head regretfully and told me they had not lived in the area for long. When she brought me out an afternoon cup of tea and a large slice of homemade fruit cake, she was beaming. 'This might interest you,' she said and produced the deeds to the cottage. I looked through the ancient handwritten entries on the deeds and came across an entry dating from the eighteen hundreds that transferred the ownership of the cottage for 'As much beer as may be drunk between sunrise and sunset in one day.' I hope that he had a raging thirst, and a more than average capacity because the cottage must be worth half a million pounds now.

If anyone asked where we were working the standard reply would not be 'Chute' but 'Off spadger catchin.' At the rear of an old thatched cottage, tucked under the eaves of the overhanging thatch, we'd found a couple of poles with iron hooks on the top. These were wrapped in a rotting old net, similar to a fishing net. We lifted them down from the iron brackets where they were hanging so we could repair the cob wall beneath with lime putty, before giving it a couple of coats of homemade lime wash. An elderly man was seated on a chair behind us, shucking peas from their pod into an enamel saucepan.

'Ere, watch my spadger tackle,' he called. We looked blank, and he heaved himself off the chair and came over to explain that he used the nets and poles to catch sparrows. 'Why?' I enquired. He looked at me in disbelief and then seeing that I was genuinely interested, but didn't know the first thing about sparrow catching, he explained.

'See, back along there' were spadgers all over the option, varmints were a getting' in the thatch an' pullin' it t' bits an' eatin' more out the gardin' than what we were, they was a regular torment to the cottagers and farmer when they roosted up in the thatch us used to pull the net over and beat the thatch wi' t' poles 'till they flew inter the net see.'

I nodded encouragement for him to continue.

'Twer'n't just I doin' it, there was lots of us, helped kip the varmints down an' give us a right tasty meal an' all.'

He explained that they would bake the sparrows in a pie, the only disadvantage being the little sharp bones. This would have seemed to be common until the period between the wars and no doubt formed a useful supplement to the rural diet. I remember eating rook. There would be a rook shoot just after the young rooks were first fledged. There were so many that instead of plucking them, we peeled the skin off with the feathers still attached, and we just used the meat from the breast in the pie. More recently I have prepared pigeons the same way, delicious it is too—apologies to vegetarians. The bird population was far greater than it is now, the dawn chorus is a pale imitation of the clamour of the past that would force visitors from the town to sleep with the window shut and go home protesting that the country was far too noisy for them. I have heard many reasons for the decline in birdlife and sparrows have become comparatively rare. Please believe me they were not all baked in a pie.

28

Bridge Over Troubled Waters

It was one of those perfect September mornings. The morning had been almost cold enough to need a pullover to wear, and there had been a faint mist that the early sun coloured to a golden glow. The sky at this time of year lacks the vivid blue of summer and turns the colour of a starling's egg, and even the few wispy clouds high in the sky seem to lack the energy to be threatening.

We were rebuilding the parapet of an old bridge across the river and repairing the flint work. It was a slow, steady job which suited the day perfectly. Between mellow old brick piers there were panels of knapped flints that were chipped almost square to enable them to be set into decorative panels. Harry and I were using lime mortar in the same way that the bridge was built about two hundred and fifty years before. The bridge crossed a feeder stream to the River Anton, which was really just a chalk stream itself and did not broaden or deepen much until it joined the river Test. We unrolled some hessian and stretched it from one bank to the other to catch any mortar or rubble that we accidentally dropped. The riverkeeper was rightly concerned, lime removes the oxygen from the water, and trout often have their favourite spot beneath a bridge. We recalled how a gang working on the roads stole the vicar's tennis net, stretched it across the river Test and dumped a bag of lime upstream. Legend has it that scores of trout floated up to the top and were swept downstream into the waiting net. The poachers were not concerned about the effects of lime; they took them into a local pub which had fresh river trout on the menu and converted the proceeds into good healthy Guinness.

There was plenty of trout about. Now and then a daddy longlegs, or crane fly, would do a half-hearted belly flop onto the surface and disappear into a mini whirlpool as a trout sucked them down. Sometimes there would be a silvery flash, and a fish leapt clear of the water as it seized its breakfast. One advantage of brick and flint work is the quiet, measured pace. Once a gauge of mortar is 'knocked up' there is relative peace apart from the occasional chink of a trowel. The job suited the day perfectly, as it is a strange time in September. It positively encourages laziness. Everything is so mild. The sun is warm but lacks the energy to be hot. Even the wasps have so much to eat - with all the overripe fruit, they lack their normal aggressiveness, their wings seem to beat slower, and the tone of the buzz alters. The fat old bumblebees amble through the air like mini airships with a faulty engine. Along the telephone wires, there are swifts, they sit talking about migration, but it seems too much of an effort at the moment, and they need a cold spell to give them a bit of urgency.

Not that we were skiving, we worked as fast as we could. It is a painstaking task and very satisfying, but not one that we could rush. It allowed us to talk, though, and I encouraged Harry to tell me tales of rural Ireland. He was only about fifteen years older than me, but the times he was telling me of could have belonged to the previous century, and I smiled at his tales of warm-hearted people with their reluctant donkeys, peat fires and love of a good 'craic'. He was an educated man, I have mentioned his musical abilities, but he loved languages as well and spoke Gaelic and Latin. There was an air of mystery about him, and he never enlarged on his background, but he always seemed content with his current lifestyle. He had a fantastic sense of humour and loved playing word games and holding impromptu quizzes, which he nearly always won, radiating such an air of confidence that most people automatically believed him. Today he was taking lines from songs and poetry and reversing the meaning for fun. He had just slaughtered Kipling by misquoting 'There is a great big, red-eyed idol to the south of Dogwomandon't' when Ron rolled up. 'What's he on about? Dogwomandon't! Ask me. He'm puggled.' I tried to explain, 'It's the opposite to Katmandu.'

'Cor you're just as bad, daft the pair of you,' said Ron.

Harry smiled, 'Could be you're right at that - still I'm glad that you are here Ron, we have got a problem, and sure there's no better man than yourself to fix it.'

Ron swelled up immediately, 'No problem I can't handle.'

'Sure, I was just saying the same meself, pity Ron's not here I said.' Harry looked over at me and winked. I nodded confirmation, although I had no idea where the conversation was leading.

'See we have got to point in under the arch of the bridge, and we were going to use that old punt. Trouble is, there is hardly any clearance, it means lying flat on your back and drifting under the arch. Sure 'twould be a brave man did that.'

Ron drew himself upright and puffed his chest out, 'Good job I happened along then,' he looked over at me. 'Send a boy to do a man's job, looking for trouble.'

We loaded Ron into the punt. He lay on his back and surrounded himself with tools and a bucket of mortar. I had not been looking forward to this part as I knew that whoever was under the arch was going to get covered in dust and mortar droppings. In fact, it was worse than I thought. The punt only just went under the brickwork with the wooden sides scraping the sides of the arch, but the highest point of the arch just gave room. Harry tied the piece of rope, attached to the stern of the punt, around a tree and sauntered off with an angelic smile. I could hear muffled swearing coming from under the bridge, and despite the echo chamber effect, I gathered that the intrepid boatman was having second thoughts. Then it became clear, the water level was rising, and the punt was now trapped hard under the arch. I released the rope, but nothing happened. Ron scrabbled against the underside of the arch to no avail. There was a small gap between Ron lying flat on his back and the underside of the arch, but not enough to let him sit upright.

Harry wandered slowly back down the bank, whistling, and singing the

Eton boating song. Ron was panicking now. He had visions of the boat filling up with water and sinking, and he tried levering with his feet on the bottom of the bridge. As quickly as it had risen the water level dropped and the punt shot out from under the arch and bobbed off downstream with Ron paddling away with his bare hands trying to reach dry land. Like Hiawatha on an urgent date, as Harry described it. Unconcerned about Ron, the water was only four feet deep, and the bottom was hard and clean. He could have stepped out, but he ran aground in the water hole where the cattle came down to drink, so he floundered through the sticky, smelly mud with his lips pursed and fists clenched. The herd of young bullocks clustered in the shade of an overhanging tree kicked their heels up in delight and crowded round for a better view.

Later on, Harry gave me a most instructive talk on the use of sluices in regulating water levels, describing how a few turns of the handle would release a little flood that dropped as soon as it lowered the board again. Where we were working had been part of the old water meadow system, and in times gone by, it was regularly flooded to enrich the soil. A fund of useful knowledge was Harry.

29

Three Wheels on My Wagon

I always loved harvest time, it felt different, and it smelt different. During the day the sun beat down on the crops and then in the evening when the temperature dropped the smell would seem to intensify and the enormous harvest moon rose and hung like a red globe just above a line of faint mist. In an open car or on a motorbike the change was even more apparent, and a plunge into the cooler air of a valley bottom contrasted sharply with the warm breeze of the higher land and the unexpected currents from the fields of grain.

I sometimes helped at harvest, as I had since the age of about thirteen. As a youngster, I usually had the job of stooking - this meant following the binder around the fields. I would pick up the sheaf of wheat in each hand by the twine that held the stalks together and standing them upright, leaning one against the other in an inverted V. We added sheaves, creating a little tent-type structure of about three feet long. We would move on, rubbing our inner arms where the hidden thistles had scratched them and wishing that we had paid more attention at thistle spudding time and formed another stook until we covered the entire field in lines of little golden tents. These days, giant harvesters do all this in one operation. A combine harvester reaps the cereal, then pushes the wheat into its innards where a mysterious and noisy transformation takes place. It discharges the grains down a chute into a trailer that is towed alongside by a tractor, and it tumbles out neat bales at the rear. The technicians who operate these, ride in air-conditioned splendour and monitor the computer while listening to stereophonic music and the occasional communication from their mobile phone. Gigantic clouds of dust and diesel fumes billow about, and anyone in the open is masked like an alien. At least that is how it appears to me, but no doubt I'll be corrected.

Previously a reaping machine clattered quietly around, gently cutting the stalks and tying the surrounding twine ready for us to form stooks to dry. A tractor normally powered it but was not much faster than the horses, which went before. True, hands became a little sore through gripping and lifting on the twine all day, and the inside of sunburned arms became scratched by the stalks and thistles, but it was a quiet and congenial way to earn a few bob. At meal breaks, we would gratefully sit in the shade and drink our lemon barley water, cold tea, or cider, depending on the age group. We youngsters would have a quick bite to eat at night and then congregate on the common. There was a stretch of river, fenced off to keep the cattle out, and here on the bend of the river, we would dive in headfirst. The water was about six feet deep, but it did not matter if you could swim or not because the current carried you down swiftly to where the river broadened out into shallows that rippled across the gravel, washed clean by the swiftly flowing chalk stream. The water was icy cold and almost took the breath away. But it was exhilarating, and it was possible to keep warm by swimming upstream, where a little relaxation in effort would cause the strange sensation of floating backwards.

With the time judged right, we loaded the dried stooks onto a cart by the time-honoured method of the pitchfork, and the expert on top of the cart loaded it up like the Haywain in Constable's painting. When taken back and thrashed they would load the corn into bushel sacks, which weighed two-and-a-half hundredweight. In case this means nothing to you, it works out at about two hundred and eighty pounds or twenty stone. This is five times heavier than the authorities now say that you can carry with the current twenty-five-kilo limit. Those old farmworkers used to carry them though, and they took many a bet on how fast they could run up a flight of stone stairs with one on his back. Strangely enough, no one felt the need to pay to join a gym or have a session on a tanning bed. We spent our time off not lifting and lugging if it was avoidable, and the wages were too low, anyway.

Unless anyone was there in the 50s, it is difficult to imagine the changes that have taken place. Those of us who could afford a car or motorbike, more planning was needed. The service intervals were very short, engines needed much more tinkering with, and most working people did their own repairs and servicing. The mechanical parts were much simpler; there were no heaters or complicated electrics to go wrong - not in any car that most could afford to buy. In fact, the old joke went, 'If any part falls off, the car will stop.' There were so few components that every part was essential. There were no garages or petrol pumps open on a Sunday and so we purchased fuel on Saturday. Journeys had to be well planned. Petrol pumps were not self-service, and an attendant would come out, service the petrol for you, and charge four shillings and nine old pennies for each gallon. That is what they sold, petrol and oil, no food, sweets, or cigarettes. But it was a lengthy process depending on how well you were known. There was no quick-fill, as the attendant chatted about the weather, exchanging local gossip and as many attendants seemed to be the retired fathers of the owners we could only move as fast as their hips allowed.

I spent Sundays in Dorset. I love that county, but I must say, that in those days Dorset closed on Sundays. 'How about Bournemouth', you ask? Well, Bournemouth was in Hampshire in those days, I am not sure what they did to be excommunicated and moved to Dorset, but I'm sure Hampshire wouldn't mind it on its books now. Perhaps someone in authority visited the winter gardens and spotting no life decided it was more suited to Dorset. Inland Dorset definitely closed on a Sunday, though. But in Blandford, there was a choice of entertainment. The picture house close to the market square showed the latest epic, starring perhaps Doris Day or Marilyn Monroe. If lucky, the young Bridgette Bardot would give us a taste of things to come. Alternatively, there was a café halfway up the hill - this was the choice. Hmmm...

It was possible to find a family-owned newsagent and tobacconist that opened in the morning. Still, the Sunday trading act was so restrictive that customers sidled in furtively like an alcoholic in prohibition America, asking guiltily for their News of the World and twenty Woodbine, or Sunday Express and a packet of Kensitas, for the upwardly mobile. There was no shortage of pubs, but the Sunday opening hours restricted the time to lunchtimes or evenings. There was a very pleasant pub by the banks of the River Stour, and we drove down on a glorious summer evening and sat in the garden watching the swallows dipping and wheeling and the moorhen bobbing about busily. I placed my pint on the table and stretched out my hand to stroke the head of a benign-looking boxer dog that ambled up as we sat down. He waggled his rump in delight and ignored me completely, sidestepping around and burying his wrinkled chops in the pint glass. With a practised slurp, he drained the top off my pint and waddled away, blowing the froth off his whiskers. I wasn't having this; I took the glass up to the counter and caught the eye of the landlord. 'Look, your dog has just drunk my beer.' He looked at me in the same kindly fashion that the dog had employed, 'Never you mind nipper, never you mind, Tw'ont do him no harm, he'm used to it see'.

* * *

Changes were occurring, and some pubs no longer frowned if you took your girlfriend into the public bar. Life was more colourful, and cars were appearing in bright colours and shapes that echoed the American styles. A lot of families had a television now. Bulky boxes that showed black and white images that dissolved into a flurry of spots we nicknamed 'snow'. There was no daytime television and programmes were, on the whole, a little bland, but we saw how the rest of the world was living and a massive change built. It was slow at first and in some places almost imperceptible. Many department stores sold the same goods that they had been supplying since before the war. They used the same methods too, and as everyone was paid in cash, they geared the system to this. The customer selected the goods with the aid of an attentive assistant and handed over hard-earned wages. Shops suspended an archaic system of little pots from wires that crisscrossed the ceiling, and the shop assistant would reach up and unscrew this before placing the money in and dispatching it across the heads of the other shoppers. These little containers whizzed around like demented dragonflies to a central cash office that sat like the machine-gun posts in a concentration camp. Their glass windows looking over the heads of the staff and customers. In a flash, the correct change would come buzzing back, complete with a receipt in a Victorian script. Incredible though it may seem the system worked perfectly well and relatively quickly.

At work, things were also changing. We still had a hardcore of wealthy clients though, and some of these definitely carried on the traditional manner and expected the traditional methods. Perhaps this day the methods were too traditional. We gathered at the foot of a grand flight of curved stone steps that led up to a massive oak entrance door that had warded off unwanted visitors since the upstart Cromwell had come knocking. There was a small lead-covered roof supported by ornate pillars, but the top step was the size of a suburban patio, and during heavy rain, some water could collect and seep under the door. The historical ancestors of the present owner were not too concerned because stone flags lined the hallway. The retired general who now lived there was a stickler though, no unwanted raindrop was going to violate his territory. He had happily stomped through it as a child and not noticed it as a boy, but now he was determined to do the job properly and had employed the services of an architect from the nearby market town. He was a very proper architect with a string of initials after his name, a shiny leather briefcase and a shiny new car parked in the extensive gravel drive. The General was the picture of a country gentleman in his tweeds, plus fours, and with a glossy labrador sat obediently at his brown, brogue clad feet. The architect was a tall, slim, imposing figure in a formal pinstripe suit and shiny black city shoes. Everything about this man shone. Dick, Harry and I stood in a huddle resembling the rejects from central castings attempt to stage a revival of a Hardy rural tragedy waiting to hear how the problem was to be tackled.

The General outlined the problem, and the architect nodded sagely before suggesting, with a slightly superior air that the solution was simple. We should sink the lead tray and put a thick doormat in place. He went to turn away and was no doubt working out his fee, but the General was a meticulous man. 'And what happens when the tray fills up?' he enquired. The architect paused, but only looked slightly flustered before saying, 'Oh, perfectly simple really, these chaps will fit a pipe down into the cellar.'

'Hmm, and where does this pipe lead to exactly?' inquired the General.

'Err, well now. I know, into a sort of barrel sort of thing,' flustered the expert. The General was silent for a second, then, 'Pray what happens when this barrel becomes full?'

The architect was more used to quietly working out a problem than thinking on his feet and panicked. 'One sends one's butler down to empty it', he suggested tentatively. It was too much for us, and we clung together, red in the face, with tears of mirth running down our faces. The architect was red in the face for a different reason, but the man with the reddest face was the general. He was incandescent with rage, and the Labrador remembered an urgent appointment and disappeared into the shrubbery. For a long time after this, if anyone were looking for a solution to a problem, we would wave a limp wrist around and advise that 'One's butler would sort it out.'

The River Bourne is a very quiet, well-behaved river that gently meanders through the valley and passes under mellow brick bridges. These seem designed to attract mothers and children who excitedly feed the plump, glossy ducks, and elderly men share the bridges, leaning on the parapet, and puffing on their pipes or cigarette and putting the world to right. At least they used to be. There is probably a directive now which makes it a crime to either smoke or feed ducks, although it is still legal to smoke duck, of course.

The Bourne may not really be big enough to be considered a river, except maybe in the winter when the Bourne spreads out over the water meadows, as it had on one particular February morning. It was one of those cold but bright mornings. The breath of the cattle formed clouds of vapour, and the grass crunched underfoot. 'Parky 'int it'?' Said Dick

'A'wright in the van though, these heaters are great, we'd be shrammed in the old Morris', Ron grunted. 'Soft, you're all soft. When I was a Prisoner of War...' We switched off. His stories were all designed to impress us, but privately we felt sorry for his fellow internees. To be shut in with Ron must have broken the Geneva convention. Suddenly, Eric chuckled and pulled into the side of the road. 'I'll be blowed,' he exclaimed. 'Look over there.' We followed his pointing finger to where a skein of geese swooped slowly across the frozen floodwater. When geese land on the water, they stretch their web feet out in front and use them to slow down before settling down like miniature seaplanes. These were landing on the ice with outstretched feet and sitting on their tails with wings held out to balance them. One after another, they would slide along the ice before lifting off again, with a few powerful wing beats and circling round to rejoin the back of the queue. As they went, they honked quietly and gave every sign of pleasure as if this was fun for them and not frustration at being unable to land.

It was typical of Eric to find time to enjoy a small thing like this on the way to work. His brother Larry was one of the nicest men you could wish to meet, but he was always in a rush and worried himself sick over nothing as he was also a perfectionist. He didn't enjoy himself as much either. He would worry about something and drive halfway home before remembering that he was meant to pick us up from a job and have to come tearing back. During the frantic drive, he would worry about the reception that we were going to give him, although it was never more than gentle 'mickey-taking' and arrive hot under the collar and flustered. Then red in the face and perspiring, he hunched over the wheel and drove like a maniac, worrying about what his wife would say. Kate, his wife, was a lot younger than him, probably about twelve years, which made her seven years older than me. We all liked Kate, she was slim, blonde, and cheerful, and although Larry probably drove her mad, she tried to keep him calm. She did the office work and wages for the firm and also worked part-time as a secretary for a large farm. Unusually for those days, she had her own car. It was a three-wheeled Reliant, the sort that later became known as a 'plastic pig'.

I was doing a job on the farm where Kate worked, and she gave me a lift down one morning. She drove fast, not because we were late, but out of exuberance, I suppose. Fast driving and Reliant three-wheelers define the word oxymoron. She swung around the bends like a rally driver, and the little three-wheeler lurched violently before bouncing over to the opposite side, running up the bank and flipping over on the roof. Both doors flew open, all the glass fell out of the windows, and we slid majestically along on the roof. I had one foot trapped under the seat and my hands on the fibreglass roof. As the car slid along, I could feel the tarmac under the palms of my hands and frantically did press-ups in an illogical attempt to get away from the grinding surface. Then the little car slid up the grassy bank, and I spun around as the barbed wire fence sliced through the windscreen pillars and like an aircraft landing on the flight deck of a carrier we jerked to a halt. There is always a strange silence after something like this and I was disorientated. Everything came to a sudden halt like the end of a violent fairground ride.

I frantically looked about for Kate. But I was not to worry - she was thrown out of the open door as the car spun into the field. She emerged seemingly unharmed, although dishevelled and covered in mud and greenery. I could not believe that neither of us had more than the odd bruise. There was a trail of broken glass and body trim, forming a trail down the road. The barbed wire fence had cut through the fibreglass like a cheese wire, and the car was upside down with the roof hanging off and steam pouring from the radiator. I never understand the fairer sex, Kate's concern remained with her husband. Women say the strangest things, 'Ian, do you think there is any chance of patching it up before Larry sees it? You know how he worries!'

30

A Touch of Culture

The saying goes, 'if you can remember the 1960s, then you were not really there' (Paul Kantner). Perhaps this is true if you lived in London or Liverpool, but in my experience, it did not apply if you lived in rural Hampshire. We knew vaguely that there were places known as Carnaby Street and strange things were happening on the banks of the Mersey, but life jogged on much as before in the thatched villages and market towns around us. I remember 1960. There was no sudden leap into the 'swinging sixties', just a sense that things were changing. For me, the Mini car and the E-Type Jaguar gave a taste of things to come. Fashions and styles were changing, cars were becoming more colourful, skirts were getting shorter, and there was that indefinable sense of anticipation that usually comes with early spring.

The whole nation developed a strong literary urge, Penguin books won a court case, and Lady Chatterley's Lover hit the bookshelves and bounced straight back off again selling all 200000 copies of the first run for three shillings and sixpence a copy (about seventeen and a half pence, which is the equivalent of paying just over three pounds fifty for a paperback today). The need for culture continued unabated - over two million copies were sold in the first year. All this despite the prosecuting barrister inquiring, 'Is this the type of book you would wish your wife or servants to read?' He really had a grip of the changing times.

At work, things were just beginning to change. I was now working for a long-established country builder, and very much in the traditional mould, we had a yard and office in the main street of the village. Many tradesmen had worked there for some time—a few since the end of the first World War, over forty years before. There was a joinery shop attached to the yard which would produce not only joinery items such as windows, doors and frames but also coffins. These were real solid wood coffins with brass handles, not a bit of chipboard in sight. The company also dug the graves and supplied pallbearers to carry the beautifully made coffins. The joinery shop always smelt nice with fresh wood-shavings and the resin from freshly sawn pine drowning out the smell of the old glue pot that was simmering away on the bench. Laurie was a bench joiner in the carpenters' shop, and he told stories about his First World War experiences. He was particularly fascinating to listen to because he had been an airframe fitter in the Royal Flying Corps repairing the wooden frames of such planes as the Sopwith Camel. In forty-five years, the world of aviation had gone from this to the Lockheed company setting a new speed record of over two thousand miles per hour. Still, as Laurie said, 'You can't fix one of the Boing 707s with a pot of glue and a hammer.'

The plumbing department comprised a father and son combination who used an ancient motorcycle and sidecar as transport. The son was over fifty and the father was nearly eighty, but he still treated the son like a schoolboy even though he had been plumbing for almost forty years. This was a constant source of amusement, to listen to them bickering away, neither taking a blind bit of notice of what the other was saying. One day the father, who was not a slim man, nor was he agile, got himself stuck half behind an Aga. He struggled away, not wishing to admit defeat or ask his son for help until he finally realised that help was unavoidable. 'Son, give us hand a minute.' No reply, his son was used to tuning out his Dad's voice, consisting as it normally did of unwelcome advice or unwarranted criticism. 'I said, give us a hand.' Silence. 'GIVE US A HAND, YOU BUGGER'. This provoked a response from the son. They were a strict chapel family who never swore and even cooked Sunday dinner on Saturday to avoid working on the Sabbath.

He did not even look round to see what his father wanted. 'Right, that is it. I am going home to tell mother'. And off he stomped to kick the decrepit motorcycle into life without looking to see what his father wanted.

We were in stitches, of course, but wandered over to release the trapped old Fred. His bib and brace overalls had twisted around a pipe he had sawn through. We were going to cut the strap, but Fred panicked thinking of the trouble he was already in for from his wife, and insisted that we undid the overalls and helped him out. The sight of Fred in his old-fashioned, patched combinations is one that will haunt me forever.

* * *

A lot of the work that we carried out was in the beautiful Test Valley. The river winds through villages with picturesque, thatched cottages on each side of the road, most of them then owned by the Leckford Estate, part of the John Lewis partnership. In fact, Mr John Spedan Lewis still lived in a house that our firm had built for him in the grounds of the large old manor house. It was a tranquil place to work. The cuckoo arrived as if by prior arrangement, without fail every April, and the road ran alongside the grounds of Leckford House giving a chance to admire the hundreds of blossom-laden plants.

Everything was ordered and it appeared that nothing could disturb the peace. Even the workforce looked freshly scrubbed to match the surroundings. In those days, the older joiners and carpenters always wore a tie to work and had a freshly laundered shirt and apron each day and polished shoes.

We were putting the final touches to the refurbishment of a large Georgian house on the edge of the village. It was the culmination of a winter's project, and we had retreated to the coach house to store materials and form a little mess room with planks across oil drums for a seat and an old door on carpenter's trestles for a table. In the main house, across the expanse of gently nodding daffodils, the painters were applying the final coats to the immaculate woodwork. No quick once over here, red lead primer followed by three undercoats, filled in and rubbed down with loving care between each coat before the final coat of gloss was applied.

Most of the joinery work was finished. They had renewed any rotting glazing bars in the delicate windows, new sash cords fitted and the panelled window shutters restored to full working order. The joiners were still working in the kitchen. Originally this would have contained free-standing pine units, a dresser, and a scrubbed kitchen table. There would have been several full-time staff to keep it all in order. Now in the spirit of the modernising sixties, we had 'improved' on this by stripping everything out and fitting units. Not that this was as easy as it sounds. There were no specialist shops selling kitchen units, no B&Q or any other superstore. Everything was handmade. Gordon, the joiner was one of the old school. He had made a superb job of the units, solid wood, mortice and tenon joints and every drawer with a neat row of dovetails holding it together. Now came the worktop. Each one had to be handmade, and this was finished by having Formica glued on.

This was the first worktop that Gordon had ever done. He had placed the sheets of hard laminate to the tops, crinkling his nose at the unaccustomed plastic smell as he cut and trimmed. Now he was about to glue them on. For years he had veneered wood using the hot melted glue from the same cast iron glue pot that his father had used before. Now he was about to use new technology. This was a contact adhesive made from a petroleum product. Gordon was reading the instructions and grumbling away to himself. 'Spread thic dang tackle all over both o' the surfaces and wait for 'un t' go tacky.'

'Get it wrong you'm buggered, casn't shift it arter that.' He stood shaking his head and scratching it through the flat cap that he wore in summer and winter, indoors or out. Plucking up courage, at last, he spread the adhesive on to both surfaces with the serrated applicator. Vapour rose and filled the kitchen, and the painters working in the hall outside were complaining and making exaggerated choking sounds. Red-faced and perspiring, Gordon triumphantly spread the last gooey portion onto the back of a Formica sheet and stood back. 'Coming for a cuppa?' I called to Gordon. He shook his head.

'Best stay here and watch. 'Case thic tackle goes off.' I turned away and took a couple of steps. There was an almighty WHOOMPH that rattled the windows, followed by a hoarse cry. I sprinted back into the kitchen and was greeted by a haze of black smuts floating in layers through the air. Gordon had lit a Woodbine up as he stood watching the glue dry and the fumes had ignited. There he stood, his previously white walrus moustache sticking out, bristling with shock, and festooned with a black oily cobweb. The ceiling was black too, and as I flung the door open, the drifting black smuts poured out of the door and swirled lazily across the corridor before attaching themselves to the wet paintwork. Fortunately, Gordon was not badly injured. His eyebrows grew back, and his lobster-like complexion faded back down to normal.

It took nearly as long for the complexion of the foreman painter to settle down to normal. All the hard work was ruined, not just in the kitchen but throughout the hallway and elegant gently curving stairwell. It was several weeks before he saw the funny side. He was sitting having his morning break when he looked across at Gordon. 'Tell you what, Gordie, wish I'd had a camera that day you tried to blow us up. Looked like a chimney sweep's apprentice you did never seen the likes of it before. When you say you are waiting for glue to go off, you 'aint exaggeratin. Thic glue went off with a tidy old bang.'

It will seem strange to those of you from a different generation, but there were no recriminations. It would be many years before I heard the words 'health and safety' and it was usual for people to smoke. A workman would light up in the house he was working in. Bus drivers and cabbies smoked as they drove along, and typists tapped away under a pall of smoke. It was possible to walk into a bank manager's office in those days when such places still existed, and he would think nothing of it if you lit up a cigarette. In fact, he would offer his favoured customers one from the silver box on his leather-clad desk. And the manager was a 'he.' The working person did not have a bank account, they paid us in cash, and we received the coins and notes each Friday in a brown paper packet. In my world, the working week was still seven-thirty to five-thirty each day, and we considered Saturday mornings the norm.

The fortunate had two weeks' holiday each year, but not the holidays abroad. There were no cheap flights or package holidays. The British seaside holiday was popular, Bournemouth, Bognor or Blackpool were popular, and Butlins was a real treat. It was the mid-sixties before I took a holiday abroad, and I met my announcement with incredulity from my astonished workmates. 'France! France! What do you want to go there for...'

'Wouldn't catch me going back there, they had to drag me there last time...'

'Don't reckon there's a beach in France. I didn't run up or down with bullets whistling around me, wouldn't mind, but I only joined to learn to play the trumpet.'

Several of my workmates were talking at the same time, but they all seemed to have the same opinion. 'Hang on a minute,' I said. 'How about the food?' My workmates nearly choked.

'Don't give me that, you can't eat that rubbish, full of garlic, bread and bleedin' jam for breakfast, frog's legs and snails, and that fish stew, billy bong they calls it.'

'That 'aint called billlybong, that's Australian that is,' Another interrupted.

'No, you mean boulevard, that's what that rubbish is called.' Sailor looked up. 'I knew a girl in Australia...'

'Shut up, Sailor!' Everyone had something to say now. 'You can't get a pint of beer for love nor money.'

'Eat horses they do.'

'Can't trust them.'

'Know why they plant those trees beside the road? So the German Army can march in the shade, that's what I reckon...'

'I knew a girl in France once...'

'Shut up Sailor'

'Tell you I did, hairy armpits and ankles like a camel!'

'Shut up, Sailor!'

The subject broadened out to include Germany, Egypt, India and Malaya, and they agreed France had none of the attractions of Bognor to anyone, with the possible exception of Sailor who had enjoyed varied attractions in many ports.

I tried another approach. 'How about the scenery in France then?'

'Look out the window', said Jim. I looked out at the meadow sloping down to the mist-shrouded valley. The sun was just beginning to burn the mist off to reveal the roofs below, and the church steeple stood painted a warm tint against the colder hills behind. 'That', said Jim, 'Is what foreigners will pay to see in a few years, and you're getting it all for nothing!' Sailor was sitting uncharacteristically quiet with his hands cupped around his chipped enamel mug. 'Mind you,' he reflected. 'Remember, some watches on the Arctic convoys with the Northern Lights reflecting off the icy Sea?' He became conscious of the silence.

'What?'

'It's OK, Sailor, we were just waiting for you to drag Eskimo Nell into the conversation,' said Jim.

* * *

In the building industry, many firms had a scheme that involved sticking holiday stamps onto a card. The employer would stick on one each week, and if the employee left, he took the card along to the next employer who continued the scheme. They cashed the card in lieu of the holiday. This was a real boon for workers in an industry where many remained employed only for the duration of the contract - he might have several employers in the same year. We treated National Insurance stamps in the same fashion. This led to the casual way that disgruntled workers tendered their resignation. 'Lick 'um and stick 'um,' was the traditional cry.

Not that the firm I was working for then had a large turnover of labour. Just after I arrived there, the bricklayer's labourer handed his notice in, and the foreman shook his head. 'Never stay anywhere that boy, itchy feet that's what he's got.'

'How long has he been here?' I inquired.

'About eleven years,' came the morose reply.

It was this General Foreman who called around to inspect the work regularly. He was a large bull-like figure who had difficulty squeezing himself into and out of his blue Austin A30 van. His face was red and deeply lined, and nobody had seen him smile, let alone laugh. On his head, he wore a battered trilby, and when irritated, beyond bearing, he threw his hat on the ground and literally jumped up and down on it. He would then beat it back into shape and jam it back on his head. They don't make hats like that anymore. The trouble was that we enjoyed the display so much that we went out of our way to irritate him, so it was self-defeating from his point of view. He was a deeply religious man and a member of the local chapel. This meant that he disapproved of drinking, smoking, and swearing so he was probably in the wrong job. I remember the plumber talking to him one day. 'You've never smoked then, Ernie?'

'Never,' came the reply.

'How about drinking?'

'Certainly not!'

There was a momentary pause. 'Got any kids, have you?' inquired the plumber innocently. Ernie shook his head. 'Didn't think so,' ventured the plumber.

The general opinion was that Ernie was due for a long if joyless life, despite the appearance of high blood pressure. Gordon summed it up. 'Way I sees it. God looks down on this miserable sod a sittin in the pew on a Sunday wi' a face like a fowsty beetroot an he thinks, longer I can keep him out of here the better, so 'ee kills two birds wi' one stone an' keeps the beggar down here to punish us.'

"She might look like a delicate flower" - *A Country Girl. Whiskey in a Teacup*

31

Swingin Sixties

There was once a song. The lyrics went something like this 'K –K-K Katie, K- K -K Katie, you're the only girl that I adore, when the moon shines over the cowshed I'll be waiting at the k- k- k kitchen door (K-K-K-Katie, Geoffrey O'Hara) They don't write songs like that anymore. Needless to say, Dick, the avid collector of obscure ditties, had added this to his repertoire together with his 'tears in my ears' and another Canadian song involving love bugs, mountain canyons and sweet-fever, lovesick blues. When the 'One-eyed, one-horned, flying purple people eater' song hit the charts, he was the first to learn the lyrics. Truly a connoisseur of the timeless classics was Dick.

Dick also enjoyed a pint at the local pub, and alongside a piano player, the public bar enjoyed a good old sing-song. The clientele was the customary mix of mainly middle-aged and elderly, and the songs were very traditional with a pleasant mixture of wartime favourites. The 'Wild Rover' would follow 'Underneath the Arches' and 'Johnny Went to Sleep in his own Little Bed Again Every Night'. This always amused me, as all the returning soldiers I knew, had every intention of sleeping in someone else's little bed if the opportunity arose. Be that as it may, the silver-haired matrons, who sat sipping their glasses of milk stout or barley wine, would join in enthusiastically, if a little misty-eyed.

One particular evening, towards closing time, the bar was full of good humour, nostalgia and thick tobacco smoke. A companion accompanied the pianist on a piano accordion, and they had played all the old favourites. 'Any requests Ladies and Gentlemen?' enquired the landlord. Dick perked up. 'How about K- K- K Katie?' he asked, hopefully. The reaction was immediate. The pianist leapt to his feet and with a face flushed with anger, shouted. 'Are you taking the p-p-p piss'? Most of the drinkers thought it was a rehearsed comedy routine and rocked with laughter. The ones who were not fooled were cruel enough to join in the gales of laughter, and Dick's reputation as a comedian became legendary. 'Did you see his expression? Don't know how he kept a straight face!'

My father's employer had modernized the old farmhouse where my parents lived. Not that it was modern by today's standard, but we no longer had an outside 'thunderbox' toilet. We now had running water and an Aga to heat it with. We hung the old tin bath on a nail in the woodshed, and we had a bathroom with water that came from a tap. Before this, we had a pump in the kitchen. This pump needed priming before use, with a cup full of water to seal the leather washer. If we were lucky, frantic pumping would cause a gurgle, then a gush of water to fill a kettle to boil for washing or drinking purposes.

Wash days involved a lengthy trip to the outhouse and started with lighting a fire under the copper. The copper was filled with water from the reluctant pump, and when the water was hot enough, the clothes dumped in. After a good pounding with a wooden stirring stick, my mother lifted the clothes out with a pair of wooden tongs, transferred them to the tin tub and rubbed up the sodden garments up and down a corrugated washboard—a miserable cold process in the winter, and a stifling hot one in the summer.

Lonnie Donegan used one of these boards to play his 'skiffle' on. Disencumbered, and finally released from some washday drudgery, there must have been hundreds of redundant washboards about then, as grateful housewives discovered the luxury of the electric 'Burko boiler.' In these pre-washing machine days, a mangle was still used to wring out wet clothes, no matter how we heated the water. Made of cast iron, with two wooden rollers, my mother turned the mangle by hand, with a cranked iron handle resembling ancient instruments of torture. In wet weather, the clothes were a nightmare to dry unless you were fortunate enough to have a good stove and plenty of room. Unsurprisingly, it was the dream of every woman to update 'her washhouse,' and although it took a while, across the countryside, households discarded mangles, pumps and coppers. Rayburns and Aga's shortly followed these, as central heating became widely available...

Recently while looking around an upmarket garden centre. There, proudly displayed with price tags large enough to make my eyes water, were the pumps, coppers, and mangles that we had discarded so thankfully. There was also a massive display of barbeques and outside cooking appliances. I had a quiet chuckle at the octogenarian who shook his head and said, "T'is all back to front, we used to go inside to eat an' outside to crap."

By the mid-sixties, the swinging sixties had yet to touch upon our corner of the country, life had already steadied for me. By the time that I was twenty, I had been working for five years, had a little money saved up and enjoyed the lanes of Hampshire in my red sports car. Now engaged, Mary had a work-transfer from Blandford to Andover and came to lodge in a cottage directly opposite my house. Her landlady was a retired headmistress and was everything you imagine a cartoon of a Victorian schoolmistress to be. Sporting a severe grey bun, she donned a high-necked frilly collar, cameo brooch and steel-rimmed, pinz-nez glasses. This formidable lady stood about five feet tall and had a truly remarkable bosom. Not separate, defined bosoms, mind, but one over-stuffed Victorian roll of upholstered embroidery. She would have inspired awe in the wildest subject of Imperial Britain. Heaven knows what she did to schoolboys. One glare from her steely eyes would have stopped a charging rhino.

When calling in on Mary one day, an appetising smell of cooking greeted me. 'Young man, I am preparing some chutney and preservatives for the church fete'. Mary's self-appointed guardian ushered me through as though I visited her. 'Perhaps you would be kind enough to take that noisy machine of yours round to the vicarage and pick up a bag of apples and a tray of tomatoes'. This was not a question. I recognized an order when I heard one and promptly set off on my errand. On my return, I humped a hundredweight of apples and some trays of tomatoes up the steps and along the garden path. She greeted me with an approving nod. 'Good, very good, have a jar of chutney. No, take two, I insist.' I thanked her and took both jars. With the speed of a striking cobra, her hand shot out. 'Two jars. One shilling each. That will be two shillings please.' I paid meekly, but I must admit they were delicious.

"...They just happened" - Lonnie Donegan

32

Get Me to The Church

You may recall that I was living with my parents in the old farmhouse. Mary, my fiancée, lodged just across the road in a farm cottage rented by the ferocious, spinster ex-headmistress. We had the opportunity to rent a cottage on the next farm, this was about a mile away, separated from where we lived by the railway line and river Anton. A minor road linked us with bridges over the railway and river. Once over the bridge, you were into another hamlet. There was an old water mill on the left, and a picturesque, thatched cottage on the right. This being the home of a family with two brothers and a younger sister. One brother was to be best man at our wedding and Jane, the sister was a bridesmaid. There was then a short row of brick-built Edwardian semi-detached farm cottages, and the one we rented was the last in the row. There were fields behind and to one side with a large garden, complete with lilac and fruit trees and views over pasture at the front, with glimpses of the river through the trees. An idyllic position.

We considered ourselves incredibly lucky to rent this at the grand sum of one pound ten shillings a week (This is £1.50 in modern money). My wages then were £15.00 a week, so this was about a tenth of my wages on rent. Equivalent to less than £50 a week. If I compare it with today's wages, it's great value for money, because it would probably cost at least £200 a week to rent a similar cottage now.

Our wedding was to be a September one, and we spent the summer decorating the cottage and gardening, ready to move in after we married. Because Mary's family lived in Eastleigh, we decided the wedding would take place there, and so the wedding banns were to be read in both parishes. I contacted our vicar. He was the man who had contributed the mistletoe a few years before, but luckily, he did not recognise me. To be accurate, he wasn't in a fit state to recognise anyone.

Arriving at the vicarage, I pulled on the wrought-iron bell pull that hung from the wall outside the seasoned old porch, and after a brief interval, punctuated by shuffling sounds and humming noises, the mellow old vicar poked his head around the door. The fumes of a fine aged wine wafted out, and he hiccupped, admittedly in a gentlemanly fashion, as we'd planned for us to call and complete the paperwork. On the appointed evening, Mary, and I arrived, and the vicar ushered us into his oak-panelled study. Leather-bound books lined the walls, and an imposing old desk with a leather top stood in the centre with a chair behind and two chairs in front. The vicar picked up a large, well-worn book and bumbled about amiably, explaining that he was going to write down our details. He might have said 'dight down our retails' it was never quite clear. In any event, he never made it to the desk and sank down on the ancient carpet, opening the book in front of him.

We stood looking at each other, not quite believing what was happening. The vicar beamed up at us and patted the carpet beside him, indicating that we should join him. I was not really a church-going person, and for all that, I knew this was part of an ancient and respected custom. So, I joined him. This is how the details of our forthcoming marriage details were recorded - the prospective bride and groom lying on their stomachs either side of the recumbent incumbent trying to control a giggling fit.

So, now we had to do the same at the church in which the ceremony was to be held. Not a country church this time, but one in a town centre at the junction of two busy roads. We phoned beforehand, and this time arranged to meet the vicar at the church. I was a little concerned and wondered if perhaps we should take our own carpet for the ceremony of lying down to record the details. I need not have worried; apparently, urban churches have different traditions. This time we met the curate at the church. We guessed that he was the curate because he wore a dog collar under his black leather jacket. When we first saw him, he was sitting on the bonnet of a battered sports car, his legs encased in jeans and his winkle-picker shoes tapping time to the guitar that he was strumming. A cigarette hung from his lip, and he flicked his long black hair away from his eyes as he greeted us with a smile and the words. 'Right on, man, so you are, like, the happy couple. Groovy man, groovy.'

We didn't have time to get to know him on a personal level, although he became a cause célèbre. He made the national papers shortly after our meeting by eloping with a Nun. But we were not to worry. He must have got our paperwork in order because the wedding ceremony took place at the right time, on the right day. Although, the church burned down shortly afterwards and Mary has always looked at me with a hint of suspicion as we pass the church, now tastefully converted into a block of flats.

In every other respect, ours was a conventional wedding for that period, not accompanied by the enormous expense and fuss that most modern weddings now involve. We held the reception at a local pub with homemade catering, and friends and relatives cladded themselves in their Sunday best. Quaffing beer, sipping port and lemon, and smoking the inevitable cigarettes and pipes, they'd retell the old stories, embellishing the tales, the tipsier they became. As a family wedding, children ran happily amok, and the oldest of guests would get their second wind spurred on by tunes of times gone by.

We were to spend the first two nights at our new home before travelling down to Devon for the honeymoon and Peter, the best man and myself had a list of items that Mary wanted for our first Sunday lunch. In the morning, before the wedding, Pete and I ventured into the local market and stocked up as instructed. This took a little longer than we thought, and we did not have time to drop the groceries at the cottage as planned. This meant that we were possibly one of the few grooms wedding parties turning up at church with a basket of vegetables. We attracted a few looks and smiles, but we didn't feel completely out of place as a look inside confirmed that it was the Harvest Festival the following day. Decorated with giant marrows, leeks like tree trunks, and potatoes the size of cannonballs, we couldn't believe our eyes! No wonder market produce was so elusive, bearing in mind we were not in the villages now. Peter muttered under his breath. 'Bloody hell mate, we could have saved ourselves a few bob and a few hours and had time to go down the pub for a quick one.' I had a job to keep a straight face for the rest of the ceremony, but I'm sure my basket of vegetables was full to bursting, and twice the size when dropped back home.

Mary & Ian. 28 September 1963

33

Come the Revolution

The real revolution, as far as I was concerned, was the widespread increase in subcontracting in the construction industry. Instead of working for a fixed hourly rate, they paid a fixed price for each operation. For example, it could be so much per thousand bricks or a rate per square yard. This had the advantage of a fixed cost for the employer and the chance for the sub-contractor to earn more money - the fast ones could make a lot of money, the lazy or slow ones starved or dropped out.

Now married, I decided that it was time to earn more money and so it was with more than a little sadness that I said goodbye to my old workmates and joined the rat race. I would like to tell you of hard times spent working like a dog for a pittance under arduous, dangerous conditions. A tale of hardship, privation and suffering. Really, I would like to have told you this, it would have made a wonderful story. The reality was somewhat different. The sites were bigger. The pace was faster, but the characters stayed the same. There may have been more of them, and some were more colourful, but most days still brought the opportunity to laugh with, or at them, and vice versa.

One of the first large sites that I worked on was a development for the so-called London overspill. It would have been impossible to know everyone on-site, but on our section, we had several workers from outside the county who were staying in lodgings until the site finished. One of these was Alec. He was around forty, dark-haired, worn fairly long and a tanned, kind-

191

looking face. He kept himself-to-himself, at first, but was friendly when spoken to. Alec lived in an old post office van, which he moved around the site each night. No one realised that he was not in lodgings at first. The first sign that he thought differently to others came when his van got a puncture. It settled at one corner, and he found this disturbed his sleep, so he got up and drove a nail through the opposite tyre. The tyre went flat, and the van levelled up. Alec seemed to find this logical, and we took more of an interest in him. Some of us would call on him in the evening and found that he was a remarkably talented man. On approaching the van, the strains of classical music wafted through the thin metal walls. Looking through the misty windscreen would reveal him in a complicated yoga position, lying on his back and frequently gripping a bone between his naked toes while lifting it in a double-jointed move high enough to gnaw on it. Taped to the roof of the van would be a sheet of paper on which he painted delicate watercolours.

He always seemed pleased to see visitors and would swing himself upright to make a cup of coffee on an old primus stove. Not only was he ambidextrous, but he also used his feet to paint. He sadly told us tales of his days as a national service soldier. The army and Alec did not see eye-to-eye. He had difficulty telling his left from his right, and if anybody raised their voice to him, he just froze and was reduced to stuttering. Even the army eventually realized that he was doing his best and found him a job as a sign-writer, painting crests and insignia. He was spotted one day by an officer who said that he was a disgrace to the uniform, so after an enquiry, they instructed him to spend the rest of his time in a tracksuit hoping visitors would think he was a civilian. His last year in the army was quite happy as he spent it painting portraits of the officers' wives and children. He said that he felt like a mad relative hidden away in an attic. We assured him that this was very true.

One evening one lad called in to see him with his girlfriend, Alec took one look at her and said that he must paint her. Now, straight away. He unscrewed a door from one of the houses and painted a life-sized portrait of her on the hardboard door using a mixture of the medium. This was eventually carried off-site on the roof rack of the lad's car. I hope that they kept it; the girl was certainly pretty, but the quality that Alec had seen shone through the painting, and she appeared as a real beauty. If she still has it, it will amaze her grandchildren.

They had moved anyone else off-site, but Alec had a strange manner that authority found it easier to ignore than deal with. He was so polite and diffident that they just kept putting it off another day, until he just packed up his few possessions and rode off on a moped, leaving us his old van to dispose of.

* * *

Dick, my old workmate, owned a cottage and was thinking of selling - it was a terrace. One of three houses that lay on the road, leading to the church in the pretty village where I used to work in my first job. It took me at least ten seconds to offer to buy it. He told me it needed a lot of work doing to it; there was no drainage. A tap supplied the water in the back garden, and there was dry rot. Despite his super salesmanship, we agreed on a price, and Mary and I carried on living in the rented cottage while I did the other one up. The rot proved to be wet rot. There is a stream which I mentioned before, which runs through the village. Upon lifting the floorboards, I was fascinated to see that the river actually ran under the floor of the cottage.

When the water was at its highest, it was about an inch under the bottom of the floorboards. I was friendly with the lads who had just installed the main drains and realized that the water table was high, but not that high. I had to run the drains through the house from the back to the front, and we did most of this underwater. I dread to think what a firm would have charged. The people living opposite became intrigued and watched me wallowing around like a demented hippo until the day came when I had to dig down and make the final connection - this was nearly two meters deep. I borrowed a couple of water pumps from the main sewer contractors; the only day I could get them was a Saturday it was strictly unofficial of course. 'Don't you worry at all, sure you could walk across the Red sea with those yokes going!'

Saturday dawned bright and sunny, and I started early, dropping the ends of the massive pipes into the deep muddy water of my front. With a satisfying gurgle then a massive belch, a steady torrent of water poured off down the road, forming a little stream of my own that I knew would flow back into the river. The prediction was accurate. Despite the best attempts of the river to flood my trench, the powerful pumps kept ahead of the flow. Marion and Don from the shop opposite waved and cheered as I dived down the hole and made the final connection.

Harrumph!! Pfftttt!!!! I heard a strange sound. A sort of snorting and a pawing of what could be frantic hooves. Arghhhh!! Harrumph! Snort! Surely, I was hallucinating as there were no water buffalo in Hampshire. Looking up, I saw an irate figure in flannels, blazer and a Panama hat performing what must have been a war dance, but in three inches of muddy water. He was purple in the face and virtually incoherent with rage. WHA...WHA...FL...FL...Through the stutters, gasps and garbled ramblings, I deciphered 'flower show' and 'horsewhip', but before he completely blew a gasket, our neighbours led him into the house opposite and poured a large scotch. As he calmed down the situation became clear. I had forgotten the entrance to the sports field and overlooked the fact that the field was a little under road level. There was a slight slope down over a flat bridge with two low walls on either side. My diverted river had found the lowest point, of course, crossing the low bridge and flooding the field. It had missed the river completely, forming a 'pond'. In any event, the water had all gone by the time the flower show opened, but it was muddy enough to give an insight into the Glastonbury music festival. Now that definitely belonged to the next era...

But here was I, self-employed, a married property owner, and about to become a father for the first time. We'd just reached the mid-60s, and since childhood, a constant in my life had been the valleys and villages that I called home.

About the Author

Ian lives in Wiltshire with Mary and his beloved dog. He is a keen amateur photographer and has won many awards for his nature, and landscape photography. He still spends many hours enjoying the stunning countryside in and around the Test Valley, and Chilbolton Cow Common.

Printed in Great Britain
by Amazon